Raindrops to Riches

Baron Alexander

Wilderwick Press

Forest Row, United Kingdom

Baron Alexander/Wilderwick Press
Unit 4 Ashdown Court, Lewes Road
Forest Row, East Sussex, RH18 5EZ
United Kingdom
www.baronalexanderbooks.com

Publisher's Note: This is a work of fiction. Names, characters, places, and incidents are a product of the author's imagination. Locales and public names are sometimes used for atmospheric purposes. Any resemblance to actual people, living or dead, or to businesses, companies, events, institutions, or locales is completely coincidental. Any slights of people or organisations are unintentional. Readers should use their own judgement and/or consult a financial expert for specific applications to their individual situations.

Baron's books are available at special discounts for bulk purchases for sales promotions or corporate use. Special editions, including personalized covers, excerpts of existing books, or books with corporate logos, can be created in large quantities for special needs. For more information, contact Baron on +44 7747 843 076 or baron@baronalexanderbooks.com

Raindrops to Riches / Baron Alexander. -- 1st ed.

Dedication

To my grandparents who fled Europe.
To my parents who rooted in Canada.
To my wife who opened my eyes.
And to my grandchildren, who make it all worthwhile.

Introduction

I was born poor. I got rich.

I got richer. Then poorer.

I got wise. I became wealthy.

This book was borne from the simple question: "what exactly is money"? My friend had just turned fifty. His kids had flown the coup. He was no-one's fool. A family man who loved his wife, loved to fish, and worked his entire life. He read the books, watched the videos. Why wasn't he rich?

The answer lies within.

Baron Alexander
St Helier, Jersey, CI
September 2022

CONTENTS

Chapter One

The Scream

A scream. A child's. No question about it. My head instinctively swiveled left to look at the endless pines that slanted upwards to a snow-capped mountain. Then, right, to the fast-running stream, the odd block of ice floating in it from the late thaw.

Again. Panic. Not the scream for more candy. The scream of real danger. Terror.

I squared myself to the rushing water and scanned across the narrow gap to the other side. It also rose towards a white peak in the far distance. I shrugged my shoulders and dropped my pack. I couldn't see anything and my neck was suddenly tight against my clothing.

I walked closer to the water. It lacked the smell of organic decay this time of year. Just the crisp coolness that followed a long winter. Downstream, I saw rocks above the whitening water. I could see the bottom from where I stood. It was the turquois colour of glacier run-off. Anyone in it would be dead in short order. I heard a helicopter fly over me and my eyes caught a glimpse of it.

Then I saw her.

Her neck was above the torrent and her arms flayed but her voice was still strong. The wind must have carried her earlier cries.

I was in the water before I knew what I was doing. It reached above my waist, clawing at my solar plexus. I leaned into the water, bracing my hiking boots on the stones below. She was approaching at speed.

My hand still held my walking stick and I made myself as big as possible, stretching my arms outwards. She had one chance. I had one chance. Then... I couldn't think about the rocks behind me—the timeless wet grey that watched the seasons pass. The invisible certainty of earth watching people, animals, and plants. The rocks were a constant amidst the rush of time.

Her chin was now under water. Her bright yellow jacket, now soaked in the ice water, must have weighed a ton. She stopped screaming when she saw me. She must have heard my cry.

She locked eyes with me. She knew. This was it.

Her body knocked me over and we both went under. I had her jacket, fearful that it would come off her. Fearful that I couldn't right myself before those rocks. Fearful that I would let go and save myself. The cold was no longer unbearable. It was becoming warm to me. I wanted to slap myself to stay focused. To stay awake. To stay alive.

She struggled, making my task almost impossible. I got my second arm around her and planted my feet. I pushed her above the waterline and brought myself upwards. Only then did I realise that she couldn't have been more than eight years old. Same age as my daughter. I almost cried until I saw that her face was sagging. A blank stare met my intense gaze.

I lost my walking stick and was a good thirty yards downstream from my pack. I made my way back and ripped it open, laying her down on her side, praying that she would live. I was fearful of the blue tint on her lips. I couldn't hear the helicopter or the wind or the water. I emptied my pack on the ground next to her and found my sleeping bag. I tore off her jacket and wrapped her in it. I held onto the bundle, rubbing her arms and back through the bag. I was crying but didn't realise it. I began to pray, even though I hadn't done so since I was a boy.

Five minutes? Twenty-five minutes? I couldn't tell you. But I saw movement out of the corner of my eye as I fought off sleep. My arms held the sleeping bag which held the limp body as I shivered violently. My hair, now frozen, scraped the down-filled bag. I willed her to move, to cry, to scream.

"Is she okay?" A hand pressed onto my shoulder as a body leaned over my charge.

"Huh? Who…? What the… ?" I felt a warmth in my torso as a fresh surge of adrenaline exploded inside. My shoulders stiffened and my eyes hardened.

"We're medics. Here, let me help." She put her hand on the back of mine, waiting for me to release the girl.

I shuffled backwards, legs stiff from crouching so long. There were three more medics, all in orange jackets with yellow hi-vis stripes. There were a few logos and I could see the distinctive red and white of the hospital cross.

The four unwrapped the girl and laid her on the gurney that the three had hustled in. Only then did I see and hear the helicopter hovering nearby. It was far enough away that I didn't feel its downdraft. One of the medics looked at me as they began working on her. She came over.

"What happened?" she said, looking at me.

I told her.

"How are you feeling?" She pulled out a pen light and began shining it in my eyes. She called over her colleague.

I mumbled that I was feeling okay. That I was only interested in the girl. Was she okay?

"She is alive. Thanks to you." She smiled warmly and I felt like I was fifteen again. Her hands were tracing my head and touching my fingers. "Do you feel that?" Her smile was a memory and I looked into her grey eyes.

"I can feel your hands on my head." I said, returning her smile. My face was like concrete and I didn't understand what I said. Could I have been talking like this the entire time?

The medic spoke into a device clipped to her jacket just below chin level. Three lines appeared between her eyebrows. Two of the other medics ran towards the helicopter and brought another gurney. This time I was put in it.

I don't remember much after that. My eyes were heavy before the rescue. Eventually they must have closed and I woke up in a warm room with three light duvets on top of me. There was a fire crackling contentedly. A young man sat, reclined, in a chair next to my bed. The walls and ceiling were made of wood, like those in the very expensive cabins I had seen in movies or in Swiss chalets or millionaire retreats that people like me would clean or serve dinner in. My eyes focused and I could see photos and medals and antlers on the walls. Was this someone's home?

I pulled myself upwards and tried to sit.

The young man sprang out of his chair and came to my side. "You're up. Great. Stay there. I'll be right back."

"Where am I?" I said, but the guy was half running out the door. He turned briefly when he heard me speak but must have decided that getting the message to someone was more important than listening to what I had to say.

My head hurt. I saw bottles of water next to me. I opened one and drank it. I felt like I had run a marathon. I saw some chocolate and looked back towards the door before I unwrapped it and ate it. It was smooth and melted easily in my mouth. I closed my eyes as the magic of chocolate did its thing. I took another piece. Then, another. Soon, it was all gone and I felt my arm muscles twitch. My legs felt like moving again, as if a switch had been flipped, giving them permission to start working.

"Hello." It was said as a statement. Or an introduction. Or, I am not sure what. I sometimes think that I place too much emphasis on our first impressions of each other. I looked towards the man who now stood in the frame of the door looking at me as if for permission to enter. The young man stood silently behind him.

"Hello," I said with a barely perceptible nod. It was either an acknowledgement for him to enter or to confirm his standing. Or both.

The man strode in. His pace was confident. Certain. He was tall, but not huge, probably around my height, six foot or so. His white hair was cropped short, as was his beard. He looked like someone who could grow a full beard in a week. His hands were large and strong. Before I could study him further, he was next to me. His eyes bore through me. They were the darkest blue I had ever seen.

"You feeling better?" His voice was deep, but concerned.

"Yes, sir."

"Do you feel well enough to talk?"

"Yes." My eyes felt like dry rocks. My skull felt like it had sandpaper on the inside next to my brain. My neck was sore. But apart from that, I was fine. I pushed myself up fully with my back to the headboard and my arms on top of the covers.

"Then may I start by extending my hand to you." He put his hand in mine and squeezed gently. His hands were like concrete blocks. Mine were like a toddler's.

"For what?"

The man looked at the young man briefly before turning back to me.

"For risking your life to save my grand-daughter's." His look this time was of concern. "You do remember?"

I closed my eyes and realised that it hadn't been a dream. I looked at him again, and the room, and my hands. I touched my face and closed my eyes again.

"Perhaps this was too soon?" He raised both of his hands, palms towards me, as he stepped backwards.

"No," I said slowly. "I remember. I guess… I'm not sure what I am thinking. Yes, I remember. I've never done anything like that before."

"No one knows what they'll do when faced with a situation." He took a step towards me and was next to my bed again.

"I heard a scream. Then, I saw a person. Next thing I knew, I was tumbling in the water with her. I needed to avoid the rocks. I remember the rocks. I just had to get her to the shore."

"Well, you did that. And I am so grateful. The medics said that she had no chance without your rescue and intervention. And if you didn't have your sleeping bag…" his voice stopped suddenly. He turned his head away from me and wiped his face with his hand before continuing. "Well, let's just say that you are a hero."

I smiled. I didn't feel like a hero. I know a lot of guys who would have done a much better job in rescuing her. "I think we're even. The medics saved me, too."

He paused before looking at me even more carefully. "You don't know who I am, do you?"

I felt my cheeks flush. I looked at the young attendant, but he looked away. "I'm sorry, sir. But are you famous? I don't watch that much television."

There was another pause, then the man's face relaxed and he smiled. Possibly the largest smile that I have seen. He began to laugh and made the attendant smile. He reached over and took one of the unopened water bottles. He had to wipe his eyes and drink half the bottle before he calmed down.

"My name is Max. I'm not famous. You have made that abundantly clear. But I am rich. And I would like to thank you for saving the most precious thing that I have in this world."

I looked at Max. He was the same man with cropped grey hair and beard and with strong hands and confident bearing. He was a grandfather to a young girl who almost drowned. I looked at the room, a tiny part of some mansion cabin in an isolated part of unmapped wooded areas. He probably owned most of the mountain he vacationed on. I looked at the attendant who had run to Max before answering my simple question and who, now, stood two steps away so as not to interfere with Max's conversation. Seeing Max laugh, he laughed too.

My mind raced at the requests I could make. The mortgage I could clear. The relationship I might salvage. The daughter I could be hero to. The car that I could buy. Something that worked. Something that I could buy with the push of a button. A life changing request that would be pocket change for Max.

I looked down at my hands and then back into those impossibly dark blue eyes.

"Are you saying that you'll give me what I ask of you?"

"I am not a genie, but I can help you and I will help you if it is in my power to do so." A very slight smile crept across his face, as though he was remembering something.

"Sir," I began, trying to be respectful. "I am a normal guy. I am not stupid. And I need money like blood. But that is my everyday reality. Money, unless it is an insane amount, will not help me."

Max raised his eyebrows, looking at me patiently. He said nothing.

I swallowed as I couldn't believe what I was saying. I motioned with my hand at the room and the attendant. "I'd like you to teach me how you did it." I kept my mouth shut and waited to see what Max would do.

He remained silent for a full three seconds before asking, "Did what?"

"Get rich."

Chapter Two

So you want to be Rich?

The bacon crunched and made Sophia smile. The table was laden with fruit and breads but I was most interested in the waffles and the maple syrup. Sophia watched as I covered the waffle with the whipped butter and let it dissolve just enough before bathing it in syrup. I had moved my perfectly cooked crunchy bacon to the side plate so it wasn't affected. She copied. We both poked at the scrambled eggs; neither of us finished those.

The breakfast room had a large fireplace with a very strong heat that ensured we only wore t-shirts. Snow fell steadily on the outside deck. It was whipped violently by an unseen wind that filled our view with white. The windows were twelve feet high and triple glazed. I couldn't see a fingerprint or smudge anywhere. There were no curtains, allowing me to just enjoy the glorious oak, pine, and cedar construction.

We all wore fluffy slippers to keep our feet warm but it was unnecessary. I was pleased that Sophia hadn't fallen in the water on a day like this one. No helicopter could fly in this and I wouldn't have been walking.

Coffee was served in individual silver pots next to what looked to me like fine china. I motioned to pour but was beaten to it. The rich black coffee filled the cup and made the air come alive. Sophia giggled as I dribbled some of the liquid on my crisp linen pyjamas that I had been given. I told her that I had to do it to match the syrup stains.

"Everything to your liking?" The familiar voice filled the room. The staff stiffened and quickly pulled out a chair for Max. He was wearing jeans and a flannel shirt, worn open lower than I would have. He had a dark t-shirt underneath. He kissed Sophia and caressed the back of her head before sitting down and joining us.

"This is possibly the most stunning place I have actually even been to outside of the movies."

Max smiled and nodded to one of the young women attending to his left. His coffee was prepared. "Thank you, Mary." He took a sip, closed his eyes, and leaned back in his chair.

I watched his casual exercise of power; how his team anticipated his every move, how his world revolved around him and how easily he lived in such luxury. I thought about my life and how I could never earn enough money to cover my expenses. How I was constantly hit from left field with costs and disasters and demands on my earnings and time. How I reacted to life instead of acted.

My waffle had become a bit too soggy, and I ate it quietly. Sophia suppressed a smile as I winked at her between bites. I decided to fill my mouth with food to prevent myself saying anything stupid. In the end, Max saved me any embarrassment.

"So, you want to be rich? Tell me, what kind of rich are you looking to be?"

I stopped chewing and played with the remaining pieces of waffle in my mouth before swallowing. My eyes went up, left, right and down. It was as though my brain was trying to access a memory that didn't exist, or to answer a question that made no sense.

"I don't understand the question. I want what you have. To own a chalet mansion and mountain and helicopters and staff and everything that goes with it. Big house in the city. Holiday homes in exotic locations. Bank balance big enough so that I'll never have to worry about food, cars, family."

Max's eyes narrowed and he nodded to himself. "If you want what I have, you need more than money." He looked out of the window and then at Sophia. "I lost my wife a few years back. She completed me. Now, I dote on my children and grandchildren. The necessary balance in life isn't easy. It can't be assumed. It is as difficult as making money and much more rewarding."

I swallowed again. The taste of the syrup made we want to take another bite, but I held back. I took a sip of coffee instead.

Max hesitated, then continued. "Rich is an odd term. It isn't only about money. Having lots of money is good. It gives you a lot of freedom. It makes you feel good initially and we live in a society that values it. It is a catalyst to many things such as physical and mental health. But if you don't have your health, no amount of money can fix it. We can talk about that and other things later. You understand what I am saying?"

"I think so, sir," I managed.

"Sophia, do you understand?" He cupped her cheek in his hand and held it there tenderly.

"I think so, papa," she said. Her lips and chin were smudged with hot chocolate. A tiny piece of waffle hung delicately in her hair, unseen by her or Max. For the first time, I noticed a string around her neck with little stones on it. I made a mental note to get one for my daughter; very feminine. Classy for her age.

"Then, let me begin at the first and most important lesson in becoming financially rich." Max inhaled as if to begin his lecture, then paused. "Wait. I need to cover some other basics before we launch into the details."

I noticed that Sophia was going to get the benefit of anything he would tell me. It made me wonder at the way that many children followed into their parents' professions—doctors have children who become doctors, teachers have children who become teachers, and so on. Children learn at the knee of their parents. They are shown the tricks and the inside track to making a success at a profession. They have doors opened. Children are rarely trailblazers–unless forced to do so.

He looked at me and I wondered what was going on behind his dark blue eyes. The eyebrows that grew in every direction. The flawless skin of his face. He pursed his lips briefly before continuing.

"Business can be easy once you understand the basics. What do you need to know in business?" He looked at Sophia, then me. Neither of us spoke.

"Do you sell sand in the desert?" Max seemed to want us to engage with the conversation.

"No," Sophia said, her face flushing slightly.

"Or horse and buggy whips in New York?" He looked at me.

"No. Not if you are hoping to get rich." I replied.

"So, what is the essential thing in any business, before anything else that you do? I'll give you a clue: it can be summed up in six words."

Sophia took another sip of her hot chocolate. I fiddled with my napkin.

"Find a need and fill it," Max said.

My body was charged, like a child at Christmas about to open his presents. His solution flattened me and my shoulders dropped slightly.

"Not convinced?" He smiled. "Not to worry. This is not the important thing that you need to learn first. Once you learn the fundamentals, you will naturally find a need and fill it. This applies whether you are in New York, Beijing, or Buenos Aires; whether you are in a capitalist or communist society; whether we are talking two thousand years ago, today, or two thousand years in the future. The details may differ, but the essence remains the same."

I leaned forward, my body at the edge of my seat. Sophia struggled to look interested but listened politely anyway.

Max smiled again. His broad shoulders filled the chair as he sat backwards. His eyes looked into the storm outside and back to me. The fire crackled loudly and we both glanced in its direction.

"Before I get into it, I want you to understand that no one fully knows money. If they did, they would be able to forecast, with one hundred percent certainty, the future values and movements of money and markets. There would be no booms or busts, no runs on banks or currencies, no unwanted inflation or deflation. There are people who *understand* money. They understand trends and can forecast tendencies but money and wealth are complex systems that operate within complex relationships. The uncertainties are too great and unknowable—partly because, as they are known, others change their behaviour and the outcomes become unknowable again."

"Like known unknowns and unknown unknowns?" I say.

"Precisely. This is why we are not going to discuss theory or tax treatment or global trends. We are going to talk about the essence of what it takes to become rich."

I nodded, trying not to look too excited.

"Never ignore or underestimate the power and importance of the other forms of wealth. As you gain financially, your time will become more valuable. You will want time with yourself, with loved ones, with friends. This may create a crisis in your business model and it is something that you will need to address in due course. Likewise, with health. Tomorrow is promised to no-one. If you don't maintain your body, it may just pack up and quit on you—like a neglected car or tool that hasn't been serviced and cared for. And many of your opportunities will be available or closed to you depending on society. I call it standing on the shoulders of giants. Our democracy and rule of law is the culmination of centuries of wars, negotiations, laws, and tradition. What is happening today will change, sometimes for the better, sometimes for the worse. You will need to apply your skills differently if you are operating in seventeenth-century England versus twenty-first century United States. Or eighteenth-century China versus today's China. How you integrate yourself within that society will impact on your creditability with your fellow citizens."

I smiled to let Max know that I was listening and understood. I thought I saw a flicker of a scowl in return. I kept on wondering what he was thinking about me as he was speaking.

"Papa, do I need to stay? This is a bit boring." Sophia turned her pleading eyes on her grandfather.

"In a bit, sweetheart." Max turned to me. "Our friend wants to know how to get rich."

I couldn't help but smile as Sophia turned to look to me.

"Forget all the history and theory. Until you are able to control your own purse, you'll never amount to much. It is the first and pivotal goal."

"Purse?" I wasn't sure whether I heard correctly. I was a guy; I didn't carry a purse or handbag.

"Wallet. Bank account. It doesn't matter what you call something. It is where you put your money and keep it safe. Accumulating it. Remember that words are both important and irrelevant with money. Look beyond the superficial label and understand what it is that you are looking at or for."

"OK."

"Now listen carefully, because this is important." He leaned forward. Sophia and I both leaned forward in turn. "Ten percent of everything you earn is yours."

His eyes looked intently at Sophia, then me. The same annoyance crossed his face, then passed.

"That's it," he said. His face reddened slightly. "Save ten percent of everything you earn. Do that, and you will have learned the first and most important lesson that can be passed on."

"But I don't earn much. And I pay taxes. And my mortgage. And my kid's…"

"Ten percent," he cut me off. His voice was firm.

"Of the net or gross? I have almost no net income, so I won't save anything."

"Gross. And pay yourself first. If you earn $10,000, set aside $1,000 for yourself. Pay your taxes, mortgage and family expenses out of the $9,000. It will be tough. Sometimes it will feel impossible. But you will do it. The same way that you live on $10k. You will make adjustments. However, now you will have saved some capital."

"That's impossible for me. I can't cut any more."

Max got up and rolled his head. "Then, that's that. If something as simple as saving is impossible, you will never be able to implement the other points. My guy will drop you off wherever you want. You can stay here as long as you want. Sophia and I are eternally grateful for what you have done."

He began walking away from the breakfast table. I watched, feeling like my boat was sinking in front of me in the middle of the ocean. When would I ever get this opportunity again? Before I could open my mouth, he was gone and I was alone with Sophia again.

Chapter Three

How to get Rich

I awoke the next day to absolute silence, apart from the muted sound of a log that slipped in the fire. It had burned down to embers and I padded over in my slippers to put another on the glowing remains. I rubbed my hands against my pyjamas and looked out across the all-white vista beyond my window. Winter was not yet done with us. It was like a snow globe but with all of the white bits sitting serenely on the branches for as far as the eye could see.

The sky was blue, nature's fury spent. A lone raven flew in search of food.

I dressed and went to find Max. I wasn't ready to leave.

He looked up from his book as I entered the library. A coffee sat on a discreet table next to his overstuffed leather chair. He reached over to it as I approached. It looked as though he was trying to hide a small grin.

"Yes, my boy?" He put his book next to the coffee and extended his hand. He didn't get up.

I shook it, then sat on the adjoining chair. The same young man who shadowed Max appeared from nowhere and asked if I wanted anything. I decided on coffee and a water. I swivelled my body towards Max and sat on the edge of my chair.

"I don't understand." It came out before I could think through my question.

His eyes betrayed the smile that the face resisted.

"How can saving make me rich? I don't even have a job right now."

Max frowned, nodding his head. "It tends to only work if you are earning. Once you get some capital, you can get it to work for you. As you know, capital begets capital…"

"So how can saving make me rich if I have no money, no job, no hope?"

"Hope is an entirely different matter. You need to keep a strong will, strong mind, and healthy body. Or else, you will never be able to complete this journey." He shifted himself to the edge of his seat. "Paying yourself ten percent is not about the money or the percentage. It is about discipline. It is about learning to say 'no' to your desires and whims. To value yourself and your time without losing respect to the others you need to also pay."

I squirmed in my chair and let my back rest against the cushions. I took a sip of my water.

"It helps if you have a job." He rubbed his snow-white beard. "But you will be surprised at how creative a person can be even without one. The key is turning yourself into a person who accumulates, attracts, and grows wealth. And the first step is learning how to save."

I put my hands up in surrender. "OK. I grant you that. What else do I need to learn so that I can eventually afford to live like this?" I let my hand sweep across the images of the books that lined every inch of the room's walls.

"The first thing that you need to have is the desire to become rich. It is the proverbial horse and water. You can take it to the water, but you can't make it drink. Likewise, with people. I can take you to the water. Whether you drink is up to you."

I tried not to roll my eyes.

"The second thing that you need to know is discipline. How to save. To live on less than you earn."

I nodded my head. His body loomed large as he remained at the edge of his seat.

"The third thing that you need to know is putting your savings and earnings to work for you. Don't think that you are rich just because you have some money in your pocket. Money is like the rain. Wealth, the lake. When it rains, it rains on everyone. Those who are wise build reservoirs to catch the rain. When it stops raining, only those wise enough to toil in making their lakes are able to enjoy the ongoing prosperity. The rain is your earnings; the lake, your savings. When others need water, they come to you. You provide it to them at a fair rate and they promise to return it to you with a fair interest. It rains again and they return their water with interest. In the interim, you have been busy increasing your lake—possibly creating another lake. You now have two lakes. The others don't bother because they know that they can come to you for their water. They argue that it is more efficient for them to continue doing what they do and let you specialise. It stops raining again and the pattern repeats. They live, some more comfortably than others; you, get rich."

The images grew and worked in my head. It seemed too simple.

"Why doesn't everybody do it if it is so simple?" I ask after a moment.

"Because it is so simple, they reason that it can't be that effective," Max replies. "People are clever. Never underestimate your fellow human. They are ambitious, happy, sad, devious, and loyal; they have every trait known to humanity. They are also busy, in love, hurt, focused, and they lack the burning desire to be rich. This is why the first step is so crucial. How wealthy you then get depends on your environment—how many shoulders you are standing on. But this is something different. I'll get onto that shortly."

"OK. We're all human. I get it. Are you saying that all I need is to want it, save it, and invest it and I will get rich?" I rubbed my itchy nose and scratched my ear.

I folded my arms in front of my chest and pushed back into the cushions.

"Yes. But it is a bit subtler than that. When you employ these truths, you become a safe pair of hands for other people's capital. They will begin to entrust you with their money."

"Sure," I scoffed. "And I'll be on the Rich List within ten years because people will throw their money at me?"

"Of course not," Max smiled. "Let me give you an example: banks handle other people's money. When they give you a loan, they are trusting that you will repay it. Do this often, and your credit-worthiness goes up. Do this widely, amongst a large number of investors, and your creditability begins to soar. Invest wisely, share your success, build your vision, and you will end up rich. Guaranteed."

"That's easy for you to say. How am I to borrow from a bank? And I make a point of not asking my friends for a loan. Do you even know what it is like to have no money?"

Max leaned back into his cushions and nibbled at a biscuit before washing it down with his cooling coffee. "I was not born rich. My father was honourable, but humble. I was born shortly before my father was conscripted. I was six when the telegram arrived at our door. It was the first time I saw my mother cry like that." Max looked down at his knees for a moment before continuing. "Of course, I had seen her cry before.

When she didn't think I was awake or looking. But this was different. It scared me and she held me tight long afterwards."

I bit my lip and reached for my coffee. I looked out the window and envisioned all of the snow that sat on the mountain and the lake that would eventually overflow with the spring runoff.

"I became the man of the house." Max exhaled as he said the words. The weight of the memory was still real. "There was a modest pension from the government and the army. There were some savings. My younger brother was only a couple of years old. We had family nearby but everyone was in the same boat." Max suddenly stood up and began pacing. One of the attendants appeared, asking him softly if there was anything he needed. He shook his head.

He picked up a log as if to put it on the fire, then thought otherwise. "It was hard. My mother got a job but she still had my brother to look after. I got a job delivering papers and the feel of those quarters in my hand when I got paid was like nothing I had ever experienced. I decided then and there that I would be rich." He turned to me. "I had passed the first barrier to entry that so many people ignore. Everyone would *like* to be rich. I *burned* to be rich. That set me on the path."

I nodded along. So many wealthy men started out with a paper route. Even Warren Buffet had a paper route when he was a boy.

"My mother made me stay in school. I'm ashamed to admit that sometimes she had to revert to corporal punishment to keep me on the straight and narrow. And I'm glad she did. A few bruises and a sore bottom allowed me to graduate and go on to get a degree in Chemistry. I still hustled. I moved on from my paper route and cut grass as well as painted homes. My mother agreed so long as it didn't affect my grades *and* I put at least half into a bank account. For what, I never knew. I did as she told me, and I eventually learned the most important lesson: how to live on less than I earned. Mother set the saving level very high but I managed to go to the movies, buy candy, and eventually an old car on the half that I spent."

I thought about my parents. They also encouraged saving but nothing like Max's mother. And it was supposed to be for something like a bicycle or my education. I never thought of it as savings to be invested. It was for things that my parents couldn't or wouldn't buy for me.

"By the time I finished my degree, I had accumulated a tidy nest egg and had created two small jobs for myself that provided me with an income. I could buy my clothes, pay for my school, and go out on the odd date without touching my savings. My mother refused any money that I offered her to help."

"What did you do with your savings all those years?" I asked.

"Initially, I put them in the bank. Then, I tried to make my money work for me. I made a lot of mistakes and I hope that you will learn from me by taking my advice. Just as I learned from my mentor. We'll get around to the pitfalls later. Suffice it to say, by the time I was 23, I was working every hour of the day and looking for opportunities. As a chemist, I ended up working for a massive company that made, amongst other things, plastic in a hundred and one different forms. I joined the company because I could see the opportunity and I wanted to learn from the best. A number of years later, I left to start my own company. I'd like to say that the rest is history, but those are the highlights. Between then and now, I made mistakes that cost me tens of millions of dollars. And I made successes that earned me hundreds of millions of dollars."

I could feel a glow from Max's eyes as he talked. He looked thirty years younger as he paced the library. His stride grew stronger and this voice deeper. He gazed deeply into the frosted forest outside our warm room.

"What was the best decision that you ever made?" I wanted to hear more about the details. Movies and books rarely set out the specifics of *how* the person made their money. They just *became* rich by some miracle. I needed to know how to create miracles.

Max swiveled back to look directly at me. A shadow passed over his face before his smile returned.

"That's easy. It was the day I asked my wife to marry me."

Chapter Four

The Three Legged Stool

Later that day, I found Max nursing a drink in front of a massive quarried fireplace. The stone was beautiful, and I could see blue hues amidst the flashes of quartz that must have been a type of granite. The metal grate that cradled the impressive logs was the size of a small bed. All of the remains glowed red. A suite of lounging chairs and sofa cuddled next to the warmth. Max sat serenely in one of the chairs, his ancient scotch within an easy reach. Outside, Sophia threw snowballs with her friends. I didn't see any of her friends' parents. The only sound I could hear was the occasional crackling from the embers and the tinkle of ice against glass.

"Have a seat, my friend," Max said when he noticed me. His body was as imposing as ever but seemed to slump in his chair.

"Thanks." I nodded as Max poured me two fingers in a heavy glass that was pushed towards me. I shook my head when he indicated ice.

"Special reserve," he said distantly. "Had it bottled specially for my wife by a distillery just outside of Crieff, in Scotland." He swirled the contents before taking another sip. "Fifty-year scotch for our fiftieth wedding anniversary." He brushed the side of his face with the back of his hand. He opened his mouth to say something but nothing came out. He looked towards the sun, snow, and Sophia outside instead.

I put the liquid gold to my lips and let it cover my tongue. I don't know if it was because I was expecting something special or because it was so magnificent. Regardless, my senses strained to capture the flavour, texture, and taste. I wanted to say something clever. All that came out was, "wow."

Max nodded and a little smile appeared. "That's what I said when I first tasted it. That's why I bought all of their 50 year old stock that year."

The two of us closed our eyes in silence and felt the warmth of the fire buffet lightly against our faces and hands. Our clothing absorbed the heat indifferently. It was a few minutes before he spoke again.

"Today is our wedding anniversary. I brought Sophia here partly because she reminds me so much of my wife. The kids will be coming later today or tomorrow."

"You genuinely loved your wife," I said. "I can only hope that someone will love me like that."

"Aren't you also married?"

"Yes," I said. "But we've hit some turbulence in our relationship. She's with her parents in New York."

"Another woman or money troubles?" Max raised his eyebrows as he looked over his glass at me.

"How'd you guess?"

"Not too hard to figure out. You are out here by yourself without your wife. Walking. Thinking about something? Trying to figure out which way to go?"

"Pretty much."

"And?"

"I think that she will be better off starting over with someone else. I can't provide for her. I can't be the husband she wanted or needs."

Max furrowed his eyebrows. "Do you love her?"

The question was unexpected. So much so, that I answered it. "Yes."

"She, you?"

"I think so. Yes."

Max pursed his lips and poured himself some more into his glass. He said nothing as he lifted it and finished it in one shot.

"Then you are a fool," he said.

I shook myself, startled.

"You have the most important leg of the stool already in place. Don't throw it away."

"Leg? Stool?"

"It's something I have always remembered. Life is like a three-legged stool. Take away one leg and the stool always falls. My three legs are family, money, and God. Not all three legs are the same for all people, but love and money usually end up being two of the legs."

I smiled at the folksy outlook of this powerful man. I could see his movements getting slower. More deliberate. He would need some coffee or a bed soon enough.

"If you didn't love your wife or she didn't love you, I understand. Keep up your relationship with your child the best you can and move on. But, if you and she love each other, then try again. And try again. And try again. True love is hard to find. It is the ultimate wealth that you will experience in this world. Everything else passes."

"I have tried," I remonstrated.

"Then try again, dammit." He slammed his glass down on the table. "You come to me asking how to be rich. Money is easy in comparison. But both need bloody determination! Never give up on your money ventures. More importantly, never give up with love. Find it, embrace it, and hold on tight."

I wanted to say that most relationships are facile and shadows of the one he had with his wife. Or that his relationship with his wife wasn't as good as he remembers it to have been. Perhaps people idealise a relationship after the death of a loved one. Perhaps he had become sentimental in old age. Perhaps the realities of dating and relationships today are much more complicated than when he was young. Perhaps society had lost its way and, with it, all of its citizens. Perhaps people simply don't have the old-fashioned values that he had when he grew up. Instead, I said nothing and nodded my head in agreement as I took another sip of his golden anniversary scotch memorial.

"You think I'm an old fool, don't you?" He said after a while. "I know that I'm sentimental but what I am telling you is real. Ignore it at your peril." He rubbed his eyes with those massive hands. I could see from this angle that a little arthritis already made his knuckles bigger. "I think I've had enough. I've got to return home tomorrow. Let's get some coffee and I'll see what else I can tell you before we have to go our separate ways."

I wondered if he was able to read my mind. I tried to keep it blank for the time it took for coffee to be brought around.

"Look," he said as he rearranged himself to face me. His coffee was balanced on his knee with his fingers lightly holding the handle. "There a million ways to make money and even more ways to lose it. Don't blindly listen and agree with me. Understand the essence of my message."

"What about the stock market?" I ask.

"What about it?" he replied.

"Shouldn't I invest in it? Every rich person has a broker who manages their portfolio, usually available exclusively to them when the company goes public. Sometimes inside information. Who knows? They are minting it."

Max's lips clamped tighter and his face grimaced briefly. "If that's what you think, you'll never get rich. Sure, people invest in the stock market. Sure, they have brokers. Just like you have plumbers and teachers and doctors. But the stock market is a reflection of values at a particular time with the best information that is publicly available. Sometimes it is overvalued; sometimes undervalued. Over time, it has represented a fair reflection of a country's economic health. As Warren Buffet repeatedly reminds us... you've heard of him, haven't you?"

I nod my head.

"It is better to put your money into a tracker fund with little to no expense than try to second guess the market. Over time, you will win. Try to time the market, and you will inevitably lose."

"So, I should avoid the stock market?"

Max closed his eyes as he shook his head. "The opposite. It is a tool for you to use alongside everything else. There is no one true path to wealth. Only the techniques are universal."

"I think I understand. Should I use it as part of my savings plan? My ten percent? Put it into a tracker fund?"

"Now you are getting the hang of it. You earn money and save ten percent (or more, if possible). You put that ten percent to work. Some people will buy a productive asset like tools or property. If you prefer, simply put your savings into such a tracker fund. But remember that it goes up and down. Don't panic; just let it stay where it is. Establish your strategy for wealth and stick with it."

I smiled at the thought, then frowned when I remembered that I didn't have a job or income. Why was I kidding myself about investing in stock markets and tracker funds and fancy talk with a billionaire who has probably forgotten what it was like to ever be poor— despite what he said.

"You don't agree?" Max was looking at me again. Could he really be reading my mind?

"All of this sounds great," I say. "I understand that I need to know my limitations and to be careful and save. But I have nothing to save. No income. How is any of this going to help me?"

Max nodded. "Let me tell you a short story about two men I came to know. Both started out with nothing at the turn of the millennium. By 2004, they were both millionaires. By 2014, one was destitute again and the other was as strong as ever."

Chapter Five

The Story of Two Millionaires

I leaned forward. "And it's true? Or is this just another parable or metaphor for me to absorb?"

Max laughed. "Unfortunately, it is very real. And versions of it happen every day in every corner of the country and, probably, the world."

"How well did you know them? What are their names?" This wasn't ancient history and I liked the idea that someone could become a millionaire in a few short years.

"I think I'll spare them embarrassment by changing their names. I won't even go into the details on the business because it is irrelevant for our purposes. I met the young man in a breakfast café when I was passing through town on business. He was still at university, if I remember correctly. He was reading a textbook and was drinking coffee by the thermos full. I commented briefly at his lack of food on the table as I walked past. He looked up, recognised me, and struck up a conversation. I still can't remember what we talked about initially. Then, like you, he asked me for some advice. I gave it to him. We shook hands and I went on my way twenty minutes later."

"And you remember him from then?" I asked.

"No. Not really. We met in the Savoy, London, before it was re-done. Around 2004. Again, purely by accident. He had heard that I was in London presenting one of our ventures at the time, solar farms, I think. He had moved to the UK shortly after I initially met him. A few years had passed and he decided to see if he could engineer a meeting with me. He called my PA and we met in the Savoy Grill for supper and drinks. He said that it was the least he could do as payment for my advice. I said ok, provided that my wife could join us." Max's face relaxed into a smile at the memory.

I knew the Savoy only by name. It was a five-star hotel with restaurants that the great and the good frequented, including movie stars, millionaires, and executives. It was within walking distance to the Embankment and, eventually, the Houses of Parliament. I hoped to be rich enough one day to stay there.

"I didn't recognise him when he presented himself to us. He stood erect, dressed impeccably in a tailored suit, and shook our hands with great conviction. He exuded confidence while still remaining humble. My wife commented to me later at how striking he seemed."

"All of that is easy when you are rich," I said, regretting it as the words left my mouth.

Max ignored my comment and continued. "Apparently, he left Canada and moved to the UK in 1998. He said that he followed his girlfriend but they broke up within two months of him arriving. He arrived with less than £350 to his name, but he did have a suit and a good pair of shoes. Within a week, he had spent most of his money trying to keep up with his girlfriend's new habits. She had relocated to London with a six-figure salary, a flat abutting Hampstead Heath, and a penchant for drinking."

I sat back and listened. I cupped my coffee and wondered how it was possible that it tasted so good.

"He searched the classified ads—everything was in paper those days—and contacted the City firms and anyone else that sounded interesting. No one was interested in him. He also knew that he needed some immediate income. He refused to let his girlfriend resent him by paying everything for him; he hoped that she would be his wife someday. He saw an ad for a secretary in a busy estate agency. He applied and got the job. The next week, he was at work earning his first money."

"On the home front, things weren't going so well. No need to go into details, but they had one argument too many and he left. On the business side, things were looking better. He saved every penny above his rent and basic living costs. He spied his first deal but realised that it was too big for him. He found a partner. It was a building that cost £640,000 with an income of £32,000. He entered into a contract to purchase the building with a 5% deposit – that's £32,000 - with the entire amount payable in six months' time. He was able to get the seller to agree this by saying he wanted the building empty. As there were tenants in the building, it would take six months before they left."

My body felt the twitch of muscles. I wasn't sure whether it was jealousy or anger. "How is this even possible?" I said. "He has virtually no income as a secretary. Where is he going to get the money to purchase? No bank is going to lend him even £350,000."

Max smiled. "This is why I said no two paths are the same. This was his path. He now had the right to purchase a property for £640,000 and he had six months to find the money. To achieve this, he put the property on the market and sold it for £1.1 million."

I gasped. "How? Those deals no longer exist, surely!"

"What this young man realised was that the four flats that made up this property had an individual value of £640,000. BUT, the building had a greater value if it was made back into a single home. He entered into contracts with another firm for £1.1m and had to wait six months to find out if the other firm performed."

"But he could go bankrupt," I said. "What happened if the company he sold the property to went bust and couldn't perform?"

Max smiled again. "These are the risks you take. Nothing is without risk. The key is to balance the caution necessary in investing wisely with the fear of losing. It is ironic. Delays lose fortunes. Delays also save fortunes. Learning to tell the difference is critical to success."

"I assume that everything went well for the young guy? Can we call him something other than 'the young guy'? Any name. Say, Picasso?"

"OK. Picasso was fortunate enough that the person he sold the property to performed and he made a very large chunk of money for himself. He looked outside of London and found property with 15-30% returns in Ramsgate and Margate. He leveraged, bought, sold, and eventually accumulated a hundred flats with an income of almost £300,000 per year. Some of these were seafront "keepers". Others were low-end rentals filled with asylum seekers and paid for by the council. One property was a school of 21 flats. He purchased it for £220,000 and sold it for £450,000 six months later. Income was £80,000 per year; he sold it because the repairs cost him more than £80,000 per year. The person he sold it to sold it on for £650,000 within a year. Two years later, he heard that it was being redeveloped and sold for £2.4 million. He wasn't jealous. He was happy. Everyone made money on it."

I didn't understand Max's excitement. "But this is hardly rich. So, he got lucky on some purchases. Good luck to him. I can't find anything like that anywhere and I've looked."

Max paused and tilted his head. "It isn't about luck. It is about being ready for when opportunity knocks. And being brave enough to answer the call. I was most impressed with the extreme savings that he managed throughout this process. He saved upwards of 80% of his income and reinvested it all. He could have bought fancy cars or been on fancy holidays. Instead, he invested. He made his capital work for him. He didn't gamble or have the usual vices of excessive alcohol and smoking. I know he enjoyed a good drink and cigar but it was always a treat for him, not a staple."

"OK," I said raising my hands again in submission. "What do I know? I'm the one penniless and he is supposedly rich. Sorry for my interruption."

"Let me fast forward through the messy details. Property in Ramsgate eventually went from £10k a flat to £150k per flat on the property that he kept. But he wasn't waiting for it. He let it work for him. In the interim, he plunged into another venture that saw him become a millionaire. With his Ramsgate property and income, banks were willing to provide him with funding for his next venture. Luckily for him, his venture went exceptionally well."

"And you're saying that luck has nothing to do with it? How does this Picasso win every time and I lose every time?" I was facing the same problem I felt every time I heard about other people's successes. I couldn't figure out how it applied to me.

"You will find that many successful people quote some version of the following: *The harder I worked, the luckier I became.* Others say success breeds success. Picasso met another man twenty years older than him. Let's call him Joe. This Joe set out a business plan that he had followed when he (Joe) was a young man back in South Africa. So successful was the business plan, that he was on the front cover of South Africa's Time magazine and touted as one of the future millionaires to watch. As it happened, he gambled away all his money—many times. Picasso met him when Joe was down on his luck and was forced to return to this winning formula."

"What's the business plan?" I asked. This is what I was waiting for. A Roadmap.

"Irrelevant for this discussion. As I said over and over again, each person must find their own way. It is the technique, the wisdom, that ensures the creation of wealth; not the specifics of one particular set of circumstances."

I could feel my body get warm with frustration. I tried to listen and poured another cup of his amazing coffee.

"All that matters is that Joe shared his plan with Picasso. They both started at roughly the same level in the new business. They each did the business plan separately, but kept in touch. They each turned the new business venture into a roaring success. Then something happened that is representative of how all of us can fail or succeed."

I was back on the edge of my seat.

"But I didn't learn about that until we met again almost a decade later. I call it his character-building years."

I nodded, not wanting to interrupt Max.

"Joe had a partner. He hated his partner. During the rise of his business, he determined that he would take and spend exactly the same amount of money that his partner took out of the business. Joe had parties at the Savoy, Dorchester, and built a home with a pool to have more parties. Joe was and is a great guy. He spent the money as quickly as it came in. What was money for if not to be spent, he said. Don't worry, I can make it back later, he said. Anyone can find £10k a month, he said. I am making £200k a month, he said. He gave £50 tips to doormen, cabs, and waiters. He always had a smile on his face and could talk to anyone from any part of society. He was smart and savvy, full of charisma."

"I'm assuming it didn't end well for Joe?" I muttered with a smirk.

"Joe ended up selling his business to Picasso for £3.5m. Tax for him was only 10% due to the structure of the sale. After tax and splitting with his partner, he had just over £1.5m. The parties continued, albeit a bit more muted than before. The 2008 financial crisis kicked in and Joe dumped most of his money into bank stocks assuming that they would rebound. They didn't. He then leveraged and bought on margin. The bank stocks languished. He couldn't hold out long enough, and eventually lost everything."

"Picasso, meanwhile, went from strength to strength. So much so, that he dealt with the rite-of-passage all wealthy people must go through: the total investigation by the tax authorities of his personal and corporate earnings. He won, and the case was closed. Then, he faced a class action lawsuit from Joe's clients--which he settled (details are unnecessary). Then, more litigation. He was bogged down for a decade with litigation that resulted from his purchase of Joe's company. He persevered. He took strategic and tactical losses and built fire walls to protect the rest of his assets. He strained to keep everything corporate and not allow himself to become personally liable. He told me that he came close to breaking a few times, but kept his head up and kept going."

"I guess it's easier when you are rich. You just get your solicitors to fight your fights," I said.

"Being rich is not just about having money. Rich is the depth and breadth of character built through adverse times. Yes, Picasso was able to pay his bills. But it was his character that kept him going. He could have quit. He could have taken his chips off the table and disappeared. Instead, he persevered and retained his good name despite the carnage all around him."

"And Joe? What happened to him?"

"This is the essence of the lesson," Max said. "Both men started roughly at the same level. Both achieved success; real success by any measure. One had the ability to save and to apply the rules of wealth. The other was set on the path to poverty. Joe now lives in a rented accommodation and can barely feed himself. Picasso lives in a ten-million-pound estate that he owns outright."

"Where are Joe's friends now that he needs them most? Will they give him back the money he spent recklessly on them? It is difficult to dampen the ego when it is successful and it is being pumped up by so many third parties. Friends appear quickly but disappear even faster in bad times. Mental and emotional strength is critical if you want to survive these types of assaults on your goals."

I sat back reflecting on his story. "Picasso started with no savings, but had a job as a secretary. He leveraged that to get a loan from the bank to purchase a property with a partner. He leveraged that to accumulate a hundred flats. He changed course and those flats continued to increase in value and provide an income for him. He started a new business, dealt with ups and downs, and ended up rich. From nothing?"

"Not nothing," Max added. "He knew the truths of how to accumulate wealth. And he had the other two legs to the stool. He found love—his second leg. He knew himself—his third leg—and was at peace with himself. The strength of self-knowledge and self-awareness cannot be overstated. It would be wonderful to have a thousand legs to your stool. You need only three to sit down or stand on it. From there, you can make yourself stronger and happier. In many ways, Picasso was already rich before he even started his journey."

"I'm not trying to be disrespectful, Max, but I'm not seeing the whole 'happily-ever-after' outcome that you are describing." The snow on the ground outside the window was piled into snowmen and I could hear the sounds of screeching as the children moved inside. I could feel my time with Max drawing to a close. "But I will try."

Max rocked twice before getting himself out of the deep chair. He stood up slowly, rolling his shoulders and neck to get the kinks out. He extended his hand, "Just in case I don't see you tomorrow. And, tonight, will be all about the family."

I shook it. A loneliness came over me as he left the room. Tomorrow, I was flying back to London.

Chapter Six

Dinner with Millionaires

The sun was going to be up well past 10 o'clock that night. My room felt smaller, more defined. Nothing was new anymore. It contained the same level of obscene luxury that I used to dream about. But now it was empty of the excitement that I sensed before. I knew that there was more to life than just money; I wasn't shallow. But, could those other things really be so important? Money solved most things in life. Ethics and happiness were reserved for those with either no money or insane amounts of money. I believed this until I had talked to Max. He said that they went hand in hand. It depressed me more than being just broke. I was now broke, unloved, and alone. And, I had no idea how I was going to construct my three-legged stool.

I pulled my things out of the closet and began packing for the flight I knew I would be taking the next day. Everything had been washed, folded and placed inside the closet as though on display at Harrods. I tried not to mess it up as I put it inside my knapsack.

A sudden screech made my head snap up and hands freeze. I waited a second, then put the clothes down and side-stepped towards the door. My senses were on high alert again. I put my hand on the door knob, when it moved on its own.

As the door opened, I saw a striking woman looking at me intently. She was a little older than me but could have passed for being in her early twenties. She wore layers of cashmere and colourful silk that sat effort-lessly on her. Her jeans belied an athletic build beneath. She stood less than a metre away. In front of her was Sophia. Both had been crying.

"I needed to say thank you," she said. Then she came forward and wrapped her arms around me. Her hair smelled faintly of expensive perfume. Her body was warm from emotion. As she embraced me, her tear-stained cheek brushed against mine.

"You're more than welcome. But anyone would have done the same." I blushed as I mumbled the words. The air was electric with her eyes on me. I as-sumed that she was Sophia's mother.

A granite-like hand grabbed my shoulder, then pulled me towards its owner. A massive man wearing a flannel jacket and looking very much like a younger Max gave me a bear hug that emptied my lungs of air.

He couldn't speak. Just patted my back with those massive hands and held me. I think he kissed my neck; it was hard to tell with his beard.

Finally, Sophia stepped forward and handed me a box that looked like a cigar humidor. "A present from my parents. I hope you like it." Her voice was small. The box was big in her hands.

I took the box and thanked her. She jumped up and hugged me as well. I felt embarrassed at such a display of emotion. I hadn't hugged my parents like this in twenty years.

"Please open the gift later. It is just a little something that we were able to get at such short notice." I glanced at the box labelled 'Patek' and put it next to my things on my bed.

"Thank you very much. Again, you really didn't need to," I said. I vaguely understood that their gift was ridiculously expensive.

"Elizabeth," she put her hand in mine. "And this is my husband, Thomas. You already know Sophia." She hugged her daughter and kissed the top of her head.

"Lovely to meet you both. You are very lucky to have such a wonderful girl. She is smart, engaging, and quite funny." I smirked at the object of our attention and got a shy squirm of her head in return.

Elizabeth's lips quivered and another tear fell silently down her cheek. "You have no idea how much this has meant to us. I hope that Max has been treating you with his usual hospitality?" She looked sideways at Thomas, communicating something that I couldn't understand.

"Max is an amazing person," I said.

"Papa's been teaching him how to be rich!" Sophia added. She jumped on her toes as she said it.

My stomach dropped as though in a fast elevator. I hope they didn't see me roll my eyes. I wished that the room would swallow me up. I waited for them to start laughing.

Instead, they peered at me for a second longer than I felt comfortable with.

"I heard that you wouldn't take a reward," Elizabeth said. "Part of the reason for the gift. I am pleased that you accepted it. But I also appreciate your request."

She turned to whisper something quickly to Thomas and shrugged her shoulders. Thomas turned to me to deliver their verdict.

"Look, we're having a family dinner tonight in memory of our mother. There will be a few more of us. They are not all, well, normal in the conventional sense. If you'd like, it would be our privilege to have you join us tonight? Perhaps we can all have a chat afterwards. Dad has made all of us suffer this conversation and journey. Perhaps you may see some different outcomes."

I looked at the three of them. I felt a shot of warmth through my chest and a tingling in my fingers. "Yes, of course. Thank you." We exchanged further pleasantries and I agreed to meet them in the dining room around 7 o'clock. I almost skipped back into my room and rearranged my clothing. I may be leaving tomorrow, but now I suddenly felt wonderful. To have been included in such a tactile love between people made me feel very special.

I began to think that Max's three-legged stool may not have been that crazy if it produced such deep love.

***

The dinner was exquisite. Max smirked when he saw me arrive and seated next to Thomas and Sophia. Elizabeth sat on the other side of Sophia and constantly held her hand, stroked her hair, and just fussed as a mother does over her only child. At the table, there were three other children of Max, their partners, and their children. Each greeted me as a hero and made me feel like the guest of honour.

Dinner lasted until after nine and the children were shown to bed. Max excused himself and I found myself sitting in the grand seating area of the log mansion. Three storey vaulted beams of wood created a space that was both imperial and intimate. Each couple cuddled up on sofas, chairs, and cushions as their eyes rested on me. At least three times during the evening I told the story of how I was walking in the woods and rescued Sophia. Parts of the story that I didn't know were filled in for me by Elizabeth and Thomas as heard by Max. Then came the time when I was able to ask a question.

"So, Max made you all learn about the three-legged stool?"

Nods and smiles as each acknowledged the truth.

"And did he force each of you to become worthy of handling wealth?" I asked a bit more warily.

Joan, a daughter of Max, replied. "You can't be forced to become worthy, you know." She giggled. "It's like the ring and those Hobbits. You can only be true to yourself. But, you can learn the rules of what it takes to make and keep wealth." Her hair had a streak of grey which was the only sign that she had aged past thirty. Her face was radiant with a quick smile and brown eyes that were reassuringly welcoming. I felt like I was in a movie set and these people were props. It wasn't possible that they could all be happy. I wanted to say something but it was too early and I hadn't had enough to drink to blurt out something like that.

Joan's partner leaned forward to add to her take on the process. Her hair was glossy black and straight and hung half way down her back. Her hands were elegant and I watched as her fingers gently touched Joan's leg or her face. She shook her head almost imperceptibly to clear the hair away, giving me a vision of health and happiness that seemed unreal.

"Not all the legs need to be about money, you know." Her teeth were perfectly white and straight, framed by her lipstick-red lips. "You need to know how *not* to lose your cash; and financial literacy is a good thing for anyone. But, Joan and I have next to no interest in money apart from its ability to keep us free from working."

I smiled. "Something the rich typically say to placate the whispering against their privilege," I said.

"Yes. You are right. We have money. I am not going to be made to feel guilty about being able to own my home or pay my bills. I can take a couple of really nice holidays a year and I don't worry about the bill when I go for meals out. Once you take that off the table, and you don't need to work, what are you going to do? Have sex 24/7? We've tried. Even that becomes a bore if it isn't shared with someone you love. Who knows, perhaps it can be done by some; not by me or Joan."

Again, her smile. I envied Joan. Hell, I envied Thomas as well. I pushed aside my memories of my own family and how I had allowed things to drift apart. How I took them for granted. How my family lacked the tactile love that I felt in the air all around me.

"Joan and I found happiness in each other, in our art, and our commitment to our community. There are people much smarter than us who can watch out for our money and ensure that it is working for us. Max agrees with our approach, I think, because it is true to us. If we had no money, we'd live the same life without the extras."

"No meals out, no holidays, and no excitement?" I suggested, trying to throw her off her ridiculous calm.

"Hardly. We would still have each other. We would still have our art. And, we'd still have our community. We might need to flip burgers or do whatever needed to be done to pay the bills, but we would be rich in the things that mattered to us."

I paused, knowing that I wouldn't go far if all I did was mock them. It was too foreign. Too easy to have great plans when you had the comfort of a rich mommy or daddy.

A heavy man with a pipe shifted his weight when Joan's partner finished. His beard was long, touching his chest, and his hair was tied back. He grunted slightly as he reached over to pat my shoulder. He was not part of the beautiful brigade. His hands were massive, like Thomas's and his father's. His skin was blotchy red. It looked as though he could have a heart attack any moment. His partner also wore her hair long, hippie style, with no makeup. She sat with her hands in her lap.

"You are a hero, my boy. Whatever nonsense you hear today, just remember that we've done nothing in our lives to compare with what you have done this weekend. We're all brats who can tell a story. We are all running on rails that others have laid down before us. No, no. It's true Joan, Tom. Let's be true to ourselves. That's what we're telling the boy, isn't it? And the truth is that we had the great wisdom to be born to our father Max. It is he who you need to learn from. We are the peanut section in this grand old opera."

His peace spoken, he exhaled, face a brighter red, and fell back into his seat. He put his pipe back in his mouth and began puffing contentedly.

No one spoke for a second before a general laughter broke out. I couldn't help but join in, despite myself. The truth had, it seems, been spoken.

"OK," Thomas said, "now that we can all agree that we'll all frauds, let me tell you a couple of stories that our father would tell us in getting across his points. As you know, there are only a few rules to the gathering of wealth. Learn those, and the rest is just detail. But, as you also know, the devil is in the detail. Never forget that almost every situation and person is different."

I nodded, trying not to be smug at the turn of events. The atmosphere felt light and airy all of a sudden. The fire burned brighter at the increase in oxygen. Each person, including myself, reached for their wine and drank. The evening was shaping up to be very interesting.

Chapter Seven

The Millionaire Son who wanted to be a Billionaire (Just like Dad)

In between the smiles and warmth of Thomas, Joan, and their ridiculously beautiful partners was a huddled man with rounded shoulders who looked at me and forced a smile. He was not like the self-deprecating blotchy bearded man. His clothes were expensive, like those of the others, but his eyes were dimmer. His hair was uncombed, and his slumped appearance made me feel uncomfortable for him. I decided to talk to him and ask him his story.

"My story?" Only one half of his mouth smiled. It was as though the sadness inside of him was too heavy for both sides of his mouth to rise.

"Sure," I replied as cheerily as I could. "If you don't mind. I don't want to pry."

I noticed the other siblings turn towards me as I spoke. Thomas rested his hand on the broken man's shoulder. I looked at the man's hands and face again. Were they brothers? This husk of a man? I then saw Joan put her hand on his other shoulder. An energy in the room changed. I felt a cold shiver run from my wrists upwards towards my shoulders. My eyes darted to examine each face in the room. No one met my eye, especially not the hulking man slumped over trying to remain part of the evening.

I was about to speak, to revoke the invocation. But he had already started.

"I was focused. I grew up on this three-legged stool stuff, but thought that it was the nonsense of rich people. I was already rich or, at least, my father was." He coughed and shook his head. "I mean, *our* father. You see, I am still so focused on myself. I'm sorry guys." He lifted his head up and smirked mirthlessly at his family who were nodding almost imperceptibly. He brushed his face with the back of his hand. I looked away. My gut was taught and my neck hurt from the strain.

"Ethics and values are the preserve of the rich, right?" He quipped with his half smile, half frown. "So, I didn't listen to our father's wisdom. I wanted to be respected as a self-made man. To walk into the banks and clubs with my head held high. To have earned it all myself. To be a *billionaire*. Self-made. Just like Dad."

My mouth went dry when I realised the type of numbers these people in front of me played with. I was interested in being solvent and, hopefully, a millionaire. They were born millionaires and were disappointed if they didn't become billionaires during their lifetimes. Each person has their own relative sense of success and failure. It was hard to watch and harder to have empathy. Poor little rich kids, my mind was saying. But this man in front of me was broken. His pain was real. The sympathy of the family tangible. I tried to park my doubts.

"Growing up, I only heard about how special I was. 'Larry, you're so special.'" He changed his voice to mock himself. "By the way, I'm Larry." He reached over and crushed my hands in his, just like Thomas had done. I nodded; I hadn't remembered all of the names over dinner. "So, when I went into a bank, they just gave me whatever I asked for. I bought anything that looked like an investment. Houses, buildings, shares, even joint ventures with my friends. I found that I had so many friends. And each one was brilliant with suggestions. They had amazing ideas and only needed capital. I had money. I trusted them. What could go wrong?"

Larry's mouth attempted a smile again, but half of it remained stubborn. His hands, pink and athletic with veins that traced the knuckles and fingers, grasped his knees. "I had never known anything except the life I grew up in," he continued. "Money was a by-product of working. It was just there. Bankers always answered my phone calls promptly. Meetings were easy to arrange with anyone I wanted to discuss my business ideas with. I built a property portfolio that included two shopping malls, a number of entire High Streets in London, two high rise buildings of luxury apartments in New York and a business park just outside of Paris. I became a founder of two cryptocurrencies, and owned three data centres. I also founded a philanthropic enterprise to deal with the very poor in India and Africa—partly to assist in the costs of death and party to facilitate micro-finance during life."

"Wow," I said. It sounded incredible. "As you are saying this, I think I saw an article on you in one of the papers. Maybe even a documentary online?"

His eyes squinted as if the memory was a glare that he wanted to avoid. "Oh, I was in a lot of articles and programmes. I made certain of it. I had a PR firm on retainer and a media guru who ensured that I was mentioned at least weekly in some forum or another. I made myself into a celebrity."

"I remember now," I said. "Yeah. Now that you mention it." I didn't want to say that Larry, the celebrity, looked like an entirely different person to Larry, the crumpled creature, in front of me.

"Anyway, things were going great until I ran out of money to draw down. I asked my father and he said I needed to take a hard look at my ventures and ensure that they were sustainable before asking anyone for any money." Larry pursed his lips and rolled his head as though he were easing some kinks out of it. "I was a self-made man, I told Dad. I guess he understood things better than I did. He told me that if I wanted to be a self-made man, then I'd need to deal with this on my own in my own way. In anger, I said I would. I also vowed that I'd never take another penny from my father as long as I lived."

The words bounced off the wooden log walls and were lost in the heat of the fire, oblivious to our conversations. I heard the sound of the grandfather clock for the first time as I waited for Larry to continue.

"It is a funny thing," Larry mused with a half chuckle, "that when you need money most is when lenders are least prepared to give it to you."

He got up suddenly and walked to the table and came back with a bowl of chocolates that he placed on the table in front of us. Each person took at least one piece as he gobbled two and then turned back to me.

"It started as an electrical current in my stomach. A premonition of sorts. A tipping point as I levelled off from my meteoric rise and I surveyed my future. There was a *chance* that I would be okay. But there was a *probability* that I would crash and burn. I decided to believe and gamble on chance. Every penny from each venture was used to plug any expenses that started to pop up as if from nowhere. Litigation by neighbours of my business park near Paris created a labour dispute that shut down the entire site for months. Just when I

got that under control, I had an outbreak of Legion-
naires Disease in the malls. We had to shut all of the
food units while we got the all-clear. Meanwhile, the
publicity reduced footfall and we began a downward
spiral on that side. We all know that property can go up
and down just like stocks. The difficulty with property
is that it is not as easy to sell quickly when the time
comes. Soon, all of my equity disappeared and the
value of the property was less than my mortgages to
the banks and investors. The *coups de grace* came during the pandemic. Commercial values fell through the
floor, footfall vanished, and I couldn't enforce any ar-
rears against tenants due to legislation. I was advised
to file for bankruptcy. Luckily, it was only corporate. I
am still solvent as an individual but I'll never be able
to raise even a million bucks ever again. My name and
credibility are shot."

I knew a lot of people who suffered during that period, chief of whom was me. I didn't know why he was
so upset. It didn't sound like he did anything wrong.
So, I told him as much.

The same half smile returned to Larry's face. "Yes,
I'm a big boy and I took my chances. I lost. Boo-hoo.
I know. I guess I am feeling foolish. That I didn't listen
to my father. That I built businesses on leverage when
I didn't have a clue about how to manage luxury apart-
ments or business parks or shopping malls. I didn't
think that I needed to. That's what managers were for.
I was the boss, right? I told them what to do. They were

supposed to manage my assets and follow the plan. The problem is that you can never and should never delegate management. Operational management, yes; but not the decisions or know-how behind the strategies and tactics of ownership. Invest in what you know. I was so proud to have survived the financial collapse in 2007 and the no-man's land over the next fifteen years. In retrospect, it was never sustainable. Or, at least, not with me at the helm."

I still didn't think he should be upset. I didn't interrupt.

"And during all of that time, did I find happiness? Balance? No. I pursued my business with a single-mindedness that I was proud of and that I pointed to as the secret of my success. Papers and articles extolled such characteristics as virtues of the new brand of capitalism. Instead, when it all collapsed, I found myself without a person I could call my friend. No wife or partner to hold my hand or tell me that everything would be okay. I was an island. A fortress. Now, I had become a failure."

Larry's eyes glistened. He spoke without passion or emotion. His story was familiar to every family in history, albeit with a few extra zeros on the end of it. Hubris precedes the fall.

"I came to realise that I wasn't special. That I was not naturally successful. And that rules applied equally to me as to everyone else." His voice had reduced to a whisper.

"Larry," Thomas said, breaking the silence, "we are all immensely proud of you. You were incredibly successful and you should be proud of yourself. I know you have heard this before, but Dad would always talk about you with such pride. He still does."

Larry's head was down and I could see a shudder of his shoulders. I looked away, trying to give him some privacy. I didn't understand why he submitted himself to this gathering if he was in such pain.

"And," Thomas continued, "we all appreciate you joining in on family get-togethers. We missed you. It's never the same without you."

Joan leaned forward, hand on Larry's shoulder again. "We love you, Larry. You get back on whatever horse you need to ride and do great things again."

Larry raised his head. "Then I wouldn't have learned a thing. Isn't that what all of this is about? I need to be more balanced. Find two more legs to my one-legged life. I've got the money thing figured out. I'll learn my lessons and do better next time. What I need is to reconnect with you guys, maybe get busy with the community a bit more. And hopefully find the love of my life."

There was a brief pause and then they all broke out into laughter.

"I love the way you make things sound so simple," Joan smiled. "You don't just find the love of your life, you know."

"You did," Larry said, with a nod to Joan's partner.

"I am very lucky," Joan said.

"Then, I'm going to start working on figuring out how to be lucky," Larry said with a full smile. This time, both sides of his mouth were up.

Chapter Eight

King Rat, A Dream

The stories continued. Thomas told me about his stint in the marines. The Hippie, I can't seem to remember his name, talked about the ashram he founded along with his wife. Joan, about the community centre dedicated to her mother and how they helped so many share their love of art. I was also struck by how the partners supported the siblings. Joan's wife—I found out that they were, indeed, married—glowed with love and pride at their shared success. Elizabeth extolled Thomas' accomplishments as well as her own while presenting them as a shared effort. Larry's whole demeanour was like a black hole amidst such positivity. I shared his sense of frustration as I was unable to secure my own three-legged stool.

Larry's words haunted me as the evening drew to a close. During a lull, he turned to me and asked, "Am I the bad guy? Did I hurt others while doing everything legally? Maybe this pain is my just punishment…"

I didn't know what to say. I was saved by Joan who rounded on him sharply, telling him that it was time to stop feeling sorry for himself. We all make mistakes and, frankly, she didn't think that he made any real mistakes. Just a little bit of over confidence. "There will be a next time," she said. She followed it up with a long hug and a kiss on the neck. I barely heard her whisper, "Just make sure that there *is* a next time, okay?"

Thomas pronounced proudly as he took Elizabeth's hand, "The personality who can build a great fortune rarely is the same as the one who can enjoy it. Conversely, the personality who can enjoy it rarely is the one who can build it." He kissed her hand in a flourish and bowed low to each of us, then floated out the door towards their bedroom. Just before he left, he added, "at least that is what Dad said…"

Mr hippie grunted as he stood up and mumbled something as he and his wife trundled out of sight, as did the rest. I waved them goodnight and sat in the quiet with the dying light of the fire and my blurred eyes. My head swam with all of their stories. I let my head fall back against the high-backed sofa. I can't recall when I fell asleep, but I do recall my dream.

KING RAT

Half an hour from the third largest city in the country, a massive grain elevator was built. It loomed large over the flat expanse of the prairies that stretched as far as the eye could see in all directions. Grey concrete roads and steely railway lines terminated in that same building. Colourful metal boxes rolled in and out on those railway lines, arriving empty and leaving full. Sombre driving men and women arrived in tractors pulling trailers or large trucks laden full of grain from the surrounding fields. They weighed their load, dumped, and left empty apart from a credit to their account which would turn into money in the bank in due course.

Very few visitors to the granary took notice of its architectural importance or the deep concrete trenches that were installed to drain away the rain and provide a barrier against the bigger farm animals coming to feed on the grain stores. This particular granary was next to a large field where cows and horses and goats and sheep all enjoyed the sweetness of the plentiful grass that grew quickly. The problem with cows and horses and goats and sheep is that they also like grain. The builders of the granary realised that if they didn't figure out a way to stop the animals walking from the field into the elevator, they wouldn't have any grain in the granary to sell. They tried fences, but the powerful aroma of the fresh grain was too much for the animals to resist. The builders devised a simple and very effective way to resolve this.

Generally, grates stopped livestock with hooves. No cow wanted to put its hoof onto a surface that could cause it to stumble or slip. But, somehow, these animals were prepared to brave the grates to get to that sweet grain. So, the builders determined that they would create a maze of trenches that would encircle the grain elevator and drain into the town's ditches which, in turn, drained into the mighty river that flowed relatively near the town but still very far from the granary. As this granary was special—it was the biggest one that anyone knew of far and wide—they decided to make this trench as much a work of art as a functional moat and security feature.

This set of mazes had troughs that were 40 inches deep and 60 inches wide. There were at least four troughs and each "wall" between the troughs was 24 inches wide. The total width of this trenching system was 26 feet, and the distance was enormous. It encircled the entire granary.

Some said that the distance of the trenches was measured in miles. Some said that the trenches were excessive and really didn't need to be large enough to drive narrow vehicles in. The builders built it like this to ensure that any flash floods or storms or any catastrophe would never touch their most valuable store of food. Some whispered that they built it this big because of the bill that they could charge to the granary's absent owners.

The trenches were built, and the granary was successful. It was busy all the time and especially so during the harvest seasons when trucks ready to deposit their grain were lined up for miles. The process of depositing grain went on 24 hours a day. During the rest of the year, things were always happening around the granary, but not to such an extent.

During the very busy seasons, grain went everywhere and the grain dust settled on everything. The trenches enjoyed a light dusting of this grain dust, but no one took any notice of it. The trenches seemed to clean themselves. Obviously, people thought, the builders did a very good job. As it didn't bother anyone, the majestic scene of the trenches became almost invisible to people. It worked. The rain must be keeping everything clean, people thought.

But it wasn't the rain that kept everything looking clean and tidy. It was the rats.

The rats didn't always live next to the granary. Their appearance in the trenches was an accident. It happened when a rat catcher was driving his big truck full of rats and accidently turned left instead of right. He almost drove into the granary, but at the last moment, he quickly realised his mistake and drove out and back onto the main road.

What he didn't realise until much later was that his back door to his big truck full of rats somehow opened up when he was turning around at the granary. The rats fell out of the truck and into the trenches. Some fell on the walls, but most fell into the trenches. The rat catcher only realised that he had lost his truck full of rats when he arrived home and saw that his truck was empty. As there was no way for him to know where he had lost the rats, he decided not to make enquiries and simply let the matter rest.

So, this is how the rats found themselves in the massive world of the trenches. They didn't know that it was a trench because they couldn't see anything more than the path ahead of them and the walls around them. Some rats that landed on the wall went down to join their fellow rats in the trough, but the rest remained on the wall when they realised that there was no way to get *out* of the trough once they were *in* the trough. What mattered for all of the rats was that there was lots of food everywhere - and that they were free.

The rats loved it. Eventually they started referring to each other as lower level rats and upper level rats. They could talk to each other if they looked up and down on each other respectively. But for the first few months, all they wanted to do was eat the grain, the grain dust, and anything else that blew into this haven of glorious, abundant food.

Because the trenches were so extensive, the rats would spread out in search of food. Like-minded rats congregated together to enjoy each other's company and conversation. Most importantly, they loved the food. It made them healthy, fat, and content. The lower levels didn't bother knowing much about the upper levels and vice versa. Everyone was prosperous. Everyone was happy.

As luck would have it, when the rat truck accidently deposited the rats into the trenches, the rats fell across all four trenches and the three internal walls. As it worked out, for every rat that fell onto the wall, 100 fell into the trench. But the rats that fell into the trenches did not fall evenly across the four troughs. For every 100 rats that fell into the troughs, 15 fell into the one closest to the field, 30 fell into the next trough, 50 fell into the trough after that and only 5 fell into the trough closest to the granary. The various rats soon became known respectively as the Fieldlings, Nextlings, Middlings, and the Grans.

For the first few months, there was no distinguishing the trench rats from the wall rats. There was food enough for everyone.

When the season for delivering grain was over, the trucks stopped coming. The granary had lots of food in it which would be shipped out in specially designed containers pulled along steel tracks. There was a big noisy engine on the front, sometimes two. They heard that it was called a 'train'. The good news for the rats was that when the grain was loaded onto the trains there was some inevitable spillage. This was a good time for the rats.

But those good times came to an end. The rats faced a period where all they could do was lick up the grain dust and search the Grand Trench, stuck in their specific trough and unable to meet their fellow rats in the other troughs. They searched and scoured over every inch of the Grand Trench—the walls, the floor, and all around the wide expanse that was the Grand Trench. For those in the troughs, times were tough. There was a lot of weight loss. Many rats died. They didn't know how they would survive. There was no way out of the trough. It was a race to stay alive. A race to find morsels of food before others. A battle to ensure that they did not become food for others.

For those on the wall—the Upper Levellers—things were different. They never ran out of food. For one thing, they didn't have as many rats competing for their food. There was an abundance—even after the trucks and trains finished coming. The smarter ones combined to form groups and began to collect and share their food. This allowed the rats who were better suited to gathering the food to gather it, while the rats who were better suited to protecting the food could protect it. All of the rats on the wall survived. In fact, they thrived.

They looked down with pity on their starving fellow rats. They didn't understand why the Lower Levellers didn't work together; why didn't they help each other? The Upper Levellers didn't realise that the same amount of food resided on the walls as on the floors of the trough. Nor did the Upper Levellers realise that they formed only 1% of the population of the lower level rats. They simply had more to share in fewer mouths.

Some of the Lower Levellers did well enough and emulated the upper level rats. The Grans did exceptionally well. They had more than enough food and began forming a system of gathering the grain and storing it in safe places in their domain, away from rain and the birds. The birds started coming in from nowhere and attacking the rats' hard-found wealth. They devised a system to store the grain and stationed guards to prevent non-Grans from access to the grain. They did this out of a natural sense of self-preservation.

The Fieldlings also did this, but to a lesser extent as they had more mouths to feed. Yet they were prosperous and enjoyed the occasional morsel from the adjoining field as well. They stored the grain and morsels of grass and even the occasional bits of manure deposited by nearby animals. They stored these precious piles in safe places for future use. Years of hunger ensured that they wanted to eat well through good times and bad.

The Nextlings and Middlings didn't have these luxuries. They ate everything that was there and eventually ran out of food three months after the season finished. It would be six months before the next trucks and trains would appear. If they didn't come up with a solution, they would starve. Luckily for them, one lowly rat was inspired and had the will to persevere.

As their fellow rats began to starve, a group of industrious rats decided to see if they could get to the top of the wall. It was too high for just one of them to jump, and there was no way for them to climb it. One lowly Middling rat eventually saw a pile of dead rats (which were piled up away from the others) and used this pile to climb to the top of the wall. Many of the other lower levellers decried his foolhardy tactics. They felt that he would die an even worse death. He was told that it would be better to stick with the world that they knew rather than risk an even worse death. After he climbed up, the remaining lower levellers ate the dead bodies out of sheer desperation. The result was that no other rats followed him.

When he reached the top, the Middling rat was amazed at what he saw. Initially, he was terrified as he looked down into the trough that was the domain of the Middlings and down into the trough that was the domain of the Grans. He hurried along the top of the wall until he came to the Upper Levellers. He tried to get them to give him some food. He was met with angry snarls and was chased away.

He carried on walking, looking down at his fellow Middlings starving on one side, the Upper Levellers around him, and the domain of the Grans on the other side. He saw a Gran and called out to him. After some explanation of the plight being faced by himself and his fellow Middlings, the Gran rat proposed an interesting solution. His fellow rats had huge stores of grain, more than they could ever eat. He was happy to lend Mr. Rat Middling (as he was known) half of his grain store on the basis that Mr. Rat (for short) would return the same amount of grain during the next "harvest" of the giants (as they all called the humans with the trucks and trains) plus 5 grains of profit for every 100 grains loaned. Mr Rat agreed although he was not sure if he would be able to provide the profit required. He had to take the risk—the alternative being that he and his fellow Middlings would starve.

Mr. Rat then went to the Middling trough and said that he had found a source of food for everyone that would last until the next supply of food came in. He explained that he could lend the Middlings the grain until the next season, BUT he needed to get all of the grain back *plus* 10 grains for every 100 grains lent. Mr. Rat could have set any terms to his starving fellow Middlings, but he figured that a fair return would at least give them a chance to pay it back.

In this fashion, the Middlings didn't starve and Mr. Rat became very rich. He brokered the grain and followed this pattern each season until he became the richest rat in the Great Trench. Eventually, even the Upper Levellers trusted him enough to broker their grain with the starving Middlings.

As circumstances would have it, another rat of the Nextlings domain found his way onto the wall between the Nextlings and the Fieldlings. He was eventually called Mr. Rat Nextling. He was greedier than Mr. Rat

Middling and tried to broker a deal where he charged the Nextlings 50 grains of interest for every 100 grains of grain. The Nextlings agreed because they had no choice. But, after two seasons, a popular revolt took place, and Mr. Rat Nextling was dragged into the trough and eaten by the Nextling mob. Whispers had eventually reached the Nextlings of the deal that Mr. Rat Middling had brokered, and they demanded the same terms.

Mr. Rat Middling found himself in a difficult position. He had the trust of the Grans and the Upper Levellers, but he couldn't get the grain to the starving Nextlings. He needed to expand his operation, and he needed to find trustworthy rats. During the next grain loan distribution, he noticed a couple of rats who had displayed loyalty and honesty in their distribution of Mr. Rat Middling's grain.

He talked furtively to them and explained how they could get onto the other walls. In this fashion, he was able to conduct his business across all three internal walls and distribute the grain from the Grans, Upper Levellers, and the Fieldlings to the Nextlings and Middlings. He called his enterprise the Middling Grain Bank and was able to establish his own stores in a safe place on the three walls—safe from the rain and birds and other Upper Levellers (who didn't seem to bother with brokerage or any form of trade at all).

Over time, Mr. Rat Middling found a wife and had a family, which he was keen to teach the virtues of honest trade and opportunity. His lieutenants also had families, and they also taught the secrets of trade, wealth, and the responsibility to the communities of all the domains. The Middling Grain Bank became the basis of strength and certainty for all of the rats as they redistributed the grain and ensured that no rat starved. It was only a matter of time before they bestowed upon Mr. Rat Middling a more fitting title: King Rat.

As you can imagine in a world full of rats, there were some less-than-honourable rats who tried to kill and better themselves through sheer violence and terror. These rats did well within the troughs and some even managed to get onto the walls. King Rat had to always act with caution and eventually felt that a greater number of rules needed to be agreed if the vast population of rats was to survive the new plague of bad rats.

Needless to say, some order and rules were established. There were always bad rats. There were always lowly rats, starving and trying to survive from day to day. There were the old-grain upper levellers who still managed to survive, but their lack of interest in work eventually led to them being reduced to menial roles. Some of their descendants even fell into the trough, never to return to their former glory (but always reminding fellow rats that they were descendants of upper levellers). Lower levellers who were dissatisfied with their lives learned to look upwards towards the sky and the upper levels. Some of those made it, many didn't.

Many of the bad rats and even the old-grain Upper Levellers preferred that the Lower Levellers stay in their place. They preferred the Lower Levellers to keep their heads down and focus purely on finding food. They wanted the "trough rats" (as they called them) to grumble, fight, and scuffle amongst themselves when things got bad—but not to have the will to lift their gaze upwards. It was in the interest of the wall rats for the trough rats to have no will to try. Without King Rat, this may have actually come to pass.

But there was a King Rat. He showed everyone what one rat with a will could do. The Great Trench was never the same again.

Chapter Nine

Returning Home, Starting Over

My eyes were heavy as the light crept in. The captain's voice was saying something and I felt my ears block, then pop. I looked outside as we passed through the clouds and the familiar patchwork of South-East England's countryside came into view. I was flying First Class and my head still hurt with the dissonance of Max's and my world. His lessons seemed infantile. I compared his warmth, smile, and unlimited wealth with my mortgage, rocky marriage, and near-bankruptcy.

I was driven home by a serious man in a shiny black car. Another gift from Max. I wondered whether I should have asked him to give me money instead.

When I arrived home and the door closed behind me, the emptiness reminded me why I went for my walk in the first place; the walk that eventually led to me saving Sophia. I opened the fridge and threw out the rotten courgettes and brown, hard lemons. The milk wouldn't pour. I grabbed a beer and opened the windows, hoping to clear the stench. There was no light on in the fridge. No heat in the house. My chest tightened and jaw clenched as I looked for the electric key meter. I would top up my account when I picked up some groceries.

I walked upstairs and dropped my bag in my room. There were pictures everywhere, appearing like phantoms, ghouls reminding me of my failures. They smiled at me, reminding me of times past, good times, fun times when we had money, each other. Everything.

It wasn't a grand home by any means. Semi-detached, just outside of a secondary city within commuting distance of London. Nothing like the home I grew up in outside of Toronto, or the one Susan grew up in near Syracuse, New York. Or where Susan took our daughter to her parents for a holiday. Part of me feared that this holiday might turn permanent.

Being broke, alone, and with no hope is not where I pictured myself when we bought this house ten years ago. Why didn't I ask Max for money? How was I going to save my way out of this? How could I pay myself ten percent of nothing?

I felt tears but pushed them back. I put the beer down and unpacked. I had a lot of time to think on my way back. Max said that he'd see me the next time he was in London. Rightly or wrongly, I vowed that I would be on track to becoming rich by then. Firstly, I needed to get my home sorted.

I used to earn a good salary. I was well off. The bank had eagerly advanced me a ninety percent mortgage and I had gladly accepted it. We started a family and the future looked bright. When things went bad, I had no savings to speak of, but enough to keep up the mortgage. I looked at the balance in the bank and calculated my plan.

No job. Few savings. Dire future. I guess it could have been worse. I had the most beautiful and healthy daughter who loved me. I loved my wife. I mused whether this would count as one leg or two?

I picked up my phone and called the bank for an appointment to discuss a loan. No chance. I emailed them and waited for an appointment. I needed capital if I was going to start doing something. I also needed a job. I heard the air exhale through my nose as my body went limp. I knew who I needed to call.

"Jay?" I said with as much feeling as I could muster.

"This is he," came back the familiar pompous voice. The public-school training made his voice sound ridiculous to my ear. But it was the accent of the educated, the leaders, the wealthy.

"It's been a while."

There was a brief pause and I swear that I could hear the smile over the phone. "Well, I guess I'd better get my jacket." I didn't reply as I couldn't understand the phrase. "Because hell seems to have finally frozen over."

I heard the laughter. I reminded myself why I called. I needed another leg to my stool. "I guess you're entitled to that," I said begrudgingly.

Jay was settling down. I imagined him wiping tears of laughter from his face as he continued. "Sorry, old boy. That wasn't fair. But, you have to admit…". There was more laughter.

"I may have been a bit apocalyptic the last time we spoke," I allowed. My mind flashed images that I pushed hard against.

"You think?" Jay said, finally gaining control over himself.

I hesitated. "I am in a bit of a pickle."

I heard a quick intake of breath on the other end of the phone. "How can I help? Money or women troubles?"

"A bit of both, I'm afraid."

"Don't say another word. I lost my best friend because of my own stupidity and hard headedness. I am going to make things right."

My throat closed up and my eyes itched. I took a moment before I replied. "Thanks, mate. This hasn't been easy."

"Don't worry. There'll be time for me to rub this in later—once you are back on form." The same laugh

that I knew so well. My best friend was back and I realised that it was as much my stupidity as his all those
years ago.

We parted ways shortly after I married Susan. The
details are irrelevant. But Jay stayed in the City and became even bigger in that world as a professional
manager of funds. The company was bought out and
Jay was given equity in the new entity, becoming rich.
We lost touch.

I took what money I had and got married, bought a
house, had a child and thought that I'd live happily ever
after on my savings. Retired life was like a dream.
Fancy cars, great holidays and restaurants. Best school
and clothes for my daughter, Diana. I had invested in
some income-producing property and thought that I
was sorted for life. Then the inevitable happened and I
had to sell my investments to pay for unexpected bills.
I still had savings but I was spending more than the income coming in. When I booked my walking holiday
and Susan booked her holiday to her parents with Diana, I had less than six months savings left. I was in a
rut and the rut was taking me over a ledge.

After meeting Max, I was able to refocus. I applied
what I had learned and started by beginning to build an
income. I could work for someone else but I decided
that I'd rather work for myself. With Jay's help, I
bought a burger van the next week and secured a location near a tube station that also had lots of pubs
nearby. I planned on getting the early morning crowd

with their breakfast and coffees as well as the late-night crowd after the pubs and bars closed. Hot, greasy food served with a smile was always something that I looked for when I was a customer. I hoped to get some trade during the rest of the day to keep things going. I would do everything. I would pay myself a salary because I would need to pay someone a salary at some point. From the gross amount, I paid myself ten percent. I put this aside. From the rest, I paid the rent on the pitch and the cost of my inventory. To my surprise, I had enough to pay the bills on the house and almost pay the mortgage.

But it was now six weeks since I had last seen my daughter or wife. They should have been back by now. Instead, I got the excuses.

"Diana is loving it here. Mom and Dad are happy for us to stay on for the remainder of the summer holidays. I hope you don't mind?" It was said as a question but there was a statement of intent. She wasn't coming home. At least, not to me and the situation I was in. The situation *I* got us into, I said to myself.

I was fortunate to be so busy. I couldn't wallow in my self-pity. I had my stock to buy, talk to the neighbouring resident who called the police the previous night, reassure the pitch owner that I was happy, probably pay another month's rent in advance, interview a guy who showed an interest in working the grill, check on his references, look at another pitch location and call the vendor of my original van that I may need another. All before the noon rush. Before I knew it, the crowds were leaving the underground and the local bars became noisy with pent up conversations unleashed. I didn't notice Jay until the gangly teenager that blocked my view finally took his three burgers from me and disappeared around the corner.

"Hey."

"Hi," I smiled. The sight of my old friend energised me. I'd been on my feet for hours. My knees were already feeling sore and my neck had lost all sensation. Gravity tugged the remaining bits of me remorselessly. Part of me wanted to close my eyes and submit to the floor that kept pulling me closer.

"It took me almost fifteen minutes to get this close," Jay said with a smile. "You must be doing something right with that grill."

"Nothing succeeds like success," I shot back. I wasn't hurting so much anymore. It was true. Whatever we concocted, it was exactly what the location needed. First night was slow, but it was busy every night since. I ensured that everything was immaculately clean. The menu was basic but classic. Burgers, bangers, chips, onions, and the rest. All for fast takeaway in a packaging that was environmentally friendly and at a price that a working person could afford. My clientele included stockbrokers and plasterers, grandparents and teenagers.

"I hear that you're organising a new location?"

"Next stop on the tube. Word is spreading."

Jay smiled as I prepared him my signature wrap. "Let's catch up when you're done. I'll find you around midnight?"

"I'll be here, cleaning up and making it ready for the breakfast rush." I knew that I couldn't sustain this pace, but I needed to get on top of my finances.

The time went fast. My muscles needed salt and rest when I served my last meal for the night. I scooped together a wrap for myself and sat quietly on the step as the night silence enveloped everything. Raucous sounds became memories, jostling bodies became ghosts. Parked and moving cars disappeared and the roads reflected the moon and streetlight equally off its blackened sheen. I opened a can of cola. The liquid hissed and abruptly returned to silence, as if apologetic for the disruption. Its intense bubbles tried in vain to separate the food from my tongue and cheeks. I let the exhaustion rest heavy on me as my mind relaxed. I leaned back and closed my eyes.

"Life is pretty good, hey?" the same voice. I opened my eyes. Jay.

"Feels honest," I replied.

"What I wouldn't give," he said, and then leant against the van next to me. I felt the van's suspension adjust against the added weight of my friend.

"You say that, but this doesn't scratch what you make," I said and stood up, brushing the crumbs and finger grease against my jeans.

"It's not just about the money. It is the whole thing."

I looked at Jay and his eyes were closed, face turned upwards towards the sky. I was going to enquire about his girlfriend but thought better of it. He never married, and he could never get over his true love, the love I knew he thought about when he drank that little too much. She married and had children; she still loved him back but couldn't wait any longer. He couldn't ruin their love by trying to hang on to it.

His head dropped forward and he smiled at me. "So, how's your wife?"

"In New York, with her parents."

"I know that," he said. "You've told me. Numerous times. I'm asking how she is. Not where she is."

My exhaustion was replaced with a warmth for Susan and Diana. I could still see Diana crawling, then her first steps, her first words, and first successful trip to the potty. Her grin as she held my fingers and walked with me everywhere. Her upraised arms to pick her up. Her first week at school. All of these images included Susan, rolling off like a polaroid camera snapping pictures in my head. All three of us were in every shot. I still remember the first time I saw Susan, when we touched hands, when we had our first real kiss. Then, there were the holidays, and marriage followed by our first home together. I shared my first everything with her. She was my first and only love.

"She's okay," I said. I wasn't sure about anything right at this moment.

Jay looked at me straight in the eyes. "Don't let it go too long." He made me feel uncomfortable. I wasn't keen on taking lessons about love from a man like Jay.

"I'll give her a call tomorrow."

"Don't make the same mistakes as me. Call her tonight. In any event, she's five hours behind."

I pinched my mouth like a prune, trying to hold back any other comments or thoughts. I was really beginning to think that people could read my mind.

I felt Jay's hand land on my shoulder and then tap gently. He nodded and walked away. Nothing further needed to be added. I reached for my phone.

Chapter Ten

Finding My Way

The evening air cleared my mind. I sat with my back to the burger van and let myself think. When looking at the three-legged stool, most people would agree that money and family are two of the three legs. The question then becomes: what is the leg that will balance the other two?

What happens when money is not the obvious leg? Living in a kibbutz or in a truly communist or artistic society would seem to obviate a person's need for money—at least for the individual within such a community. However, even those communities use and need money to interact for items outside of their control. Some physical comforts may be needed, but the need for money is not so crucial. In those circumstances, the society/grouping becomes the leg.

Likewise, with family. This has become a very fluid term and can refer to blood family or groupings that take the place of family. Whatever and however it is constructed, this becomes one of your legs. The key is to know yourself.

For me, I wanted to see Diana grow up. To witness her first steps, words, and read her stories as she cuddled in next to Susan and me. I wanted to enjoy and celebrate both life and innocence.

The final leg is determined by the individual and their path. Many paths are similar; none are identical.

Unfortunately for me, I neglected two of my three legs; probably all three. My stool failed. My life fell apart. I failed my wife, my daughter, and myself.

Three ancient Greek maxims carved into a stone column in the Temple of Apollo at Delphi were:

- Know Thyself
- Nothing to Excess; and
- Certainty brings Insanity

My balancing leg was me. I thought I knew myself, but I didn't. I lived to excess while telling myself that I didn't. I was certain in all things to the point of blindness to the other two legs of my stool. If I wanted Susan back, I needed to fix me first. I needed to rebuild that balancing leg. Growing up, I was diligent in not building a box around myself. I trained as a solicitor but never practiced. Many people identify with their professions to the point where that becomes one of their legs: doctor, tailor, actress, artist, and so on.

For some, mental health through exercise is a leg.

For me, I realized that I needed to carve out time for myself. As I write this, it is obvious. What do I do when I need to think? I walk, hike, and generally do things *alone*. I need the time and space. As an introvert, I need to recharge my batteries in a specific fashion. Self-reflection, writing, and exercise all form a part of this aspect. I realized that I needed to be true to this characteristic in myself.

For extroverts, this leg can mean social engagement, humanitarian/philanthropic activity. Extroverts charge their batteries differently to me. No path is precisely the same.

The tree's leaves rustled and I returned to the present. Jay was no longer there. The burger van was clean and ready for the morning rush. I always marvelled at the silence of one o'clock in the morning in London. I finished a second beer as my present and past collided spectacularly in my mind. My stomach was tight, as was my neck and jaw. My breathing increased as I braced myself for what needed to be done.

I fumbled in my pocket for my phone and pushed 'call' next to my wife's name. This had gone on long enough.

Chapter Eleven

The Savoy

The Savoy Hotel in London has a cramped entrance that belies the grandeur and spaciousness inside. Bentleys are parked unceremoniously alongside the pavement to allow for an in-and-out from The Strand to the revolving front doors, past the porters who guard them so carefully. Even without a sweeping drive, it manages to create an air of anticipation for those who can see more than a dead-end alley from the passing road. Perhaps the hotel's magic is its history or the confidence of the people who unfold themselves from sports cars or taxis to quietly tip the doorman as they glide into the historic hotel, or, perhaps, it is the price tag that has become capitalism's caste. People who can't afford it, don't come. By definition, those who come can afford it. An invisible hand more powerful than Adam Smith's keeps the peace. Where more than an invisible hand is needed, police are stationed within a two-minute drive.

I had never stayed in the Savoy before this night. My budget and lack of ambition denied me this pleasure. Until today.

Max's assistant confirmed that he was able to meet with me. I checked my watch. The Patek that I received from Max's son and daughter in law. Another forty-five minutes. I almost rubbed my hands on my trousers. It was the first Italian suit I had bought since before Diana was born. I bought it in the sales, after Christmas at Harrods. I told myself that I was making an investment in myself. It was the same with the shoes. I had spent a month's rent on what I was wearing. Luckily, I wasn't a renter. I was a landlord, a saver, a husband, and a father. I was lost, but now I was found.

I felt Susan's fingers gently touching my palm and then interlink with mine. I felt her warmth as her body drifted closer to me. I tingled in moments like this. She wore a beautiful dress that she bought when we were on holiday in Eze, near Nice in the South of France. It hugged her body and showed off her discreet muscles underneath. It was the dress she said she would never be able to wear again after she gave birth to Diana. She glowed.

Diana held Susan's hand as she watched the people and the room carefully. I wanted to ask her what she was looking at so intensely, but I didn't want to break the spell.

We were sat in the corner of a well-lit room, augmented by a domed ceiling light. A piano played something inoffensive within a circular cage. It was elegant but I found the image humorous. The proverbial canary playing in a gilded cage. Perhaps that is what we all are. I squeezed by wife's and daughter's hands with emotion as I gazed upon our own gilded cage.

"Started without me?" His voice held the same deep power from our first meeting all those years ago. I stood up instinctively The maître-d' nodded and backed away tactfully.

"Max," I said, as I proffered my hand. It was duly crushed, albeit gently. "Thank you for meeting us. As you know, this is my Susan." She stood up and he surprised both of us by leaning in and kissing her on both cheeks. "And this is my Diana."

Max stood straighter and gave her his hand. She put her hand in his and he brought it to his lips. He said nothing, but his face flushed slightly and his eyes sparkled briefly.

He motioned with his hand for us to be seated while holding Susan's chair and pushing it gently as she sat down. His beard was gone as was his flannel suit. He was dressed in tan trousers with a dark blazer and shirt, open at the neck. His thick head of white hair was cut short. But all I could see was his smile and there was the magnetic pull of his charisma.

We had high tea, and talked a little too loudly. Even Diana relaxed in the presence of Max. I sat across from him, so she was sitting next to him, as was Susan. I watched in awe as my daughter talked without fear to one of the world's richest and most powerful men. I watched with pride and love as my wife still remembered me in her conversation with Max. Always a little touch, or a glance to include me. I think that Max noticed as well.

"Do you shop at the same place as The Savoy?" I said as I picked up the silver teapot. It was as heavy as the one I had over breakfast in Max's cabin with his grand-daughter.

"Must have been a two-for-one sale," he said with his ever-present grin. He rarely talked about things like that. They were just there. Or, at least, he didn't make a big deal about them. I liked that about Max.

"I'll have a word with the manager," I said, still smiling as the dark coffee filled my cup. Both the tea and coffee came in similar shaped teapots.

The pianist had left long before I realised the piano music had stopped. Most of the people in the room had disappeared too. Diana had a smudge of chocolate on her cheek from the deserts. I couldn't help but think how similar she was to Sophia.

Max watched me looking at Diana. His chest puffed out as he buttoned his jacked and stood up. I looked up in surprise as I tried to take in what was happening. Did I do something to offend?

"Diana," Max started. "You are a very lucky girl to have your mother and father. And I am a very lucky man to have met your father." He turned to look at me, nod, and returned his attention to my daughter. "A few years back, your father did something for me that I will never forget. I'm sure he told you. I have a grand-daughter who is almost the same age as you. I gave her a necklace shortly before she fell into the river that day." He paused, then continued. "It was made out of a special substance called Beta Cloth. It is what they use in outer space. It had three little stones on it. One was made from actual moon dust. Don't ask me how. The second was from a meteorite. The third was a dia-mond."

He put his hand into his blazer and pulled out a small box. He looked at me briefly before handing it to Diana.

"I made another one when I heard that I was going to meet you. I hope that you like it."

Diana opened the box tentatively. There was a clasp that she didn't see at first. I let Susan show her. She pulled it out and it looked like a piece of string with three little rocks on it. She touched each stone care-fully, then ran her fingers along the string. I held my breath. I exhaled only when I saw her smile and say thank you to Max. They had a short hug and he put the necklace on her.

"I'll never take this off," she said as she continued to touch the stones.

"I'm glad you like it," Max said. "And if your par-ents will allow it, I'd like to invite you sometimes during your summer break to join me and Sophia on one of our holidays. Your parents are welcome to join, naturally."

"That's too kind," I said before Diana began her pleading. "If it is okay with Susan, it would be more than okay with me."

Susan nodded her head and the deal was done.

"We are getting old," I said to no-one in particular as I watched Diana grow an extra year in front of my eyes over our tea.

"We all get older. Only some of us grow up." Susan linked her arm in mine and leaned across to kiss me.

In all of our years of marriage, I have come to know the fifty shades of kisses that a wife gives to her husband. I looked up in a startled realization as she released my lips gently from hers. She nodded. I almost cried.

She forgives me.

She leaned in closer to me and whispered in my ear, "Now, forgive yourself."

I sat back, convinced that everyone was able to read my mind. The room zoomed in and out as I recalibrated my reality.

I felt an emotion more powerful than anything since the birth of our daughter. I glanced at Max and his eyes twinkled as though he could also read my mind. Both of us were smiling. Both of us were rich.

***

I don't remember leaving the table. I was floating on air. Susan and Diana left to visit our room and prepare for the evening. I wasn't sure what they needed, but I wasn't in the mood to interfere. I was in the land of magic and make-believe. I knew that tomorrow would be another day and I would need to continue what I had been doing. But, today, was a day of enjoyment, glory, satisfaction and relief.

Max walked with me to the Embankment. We looked over the Thames and then back towards the hotel.

"It is like a bubble, you know." He gazed into the distance and I tried to follow his gaze. I waited for him to continue. "We live our lives next to each other, rarely knowing what is going on within ourselves and even less so with our family or neighbours. The rich live cheek by jowl with the poor. There are good and bad people at every level of society. We play our part. And then it is over."

I didn't like where this was going. I had never heard darkness coming from Max.

"Don't worry, I'm not going to jump or anything. I love life. I love *my* life. I love what I am still going to do with the life I have left."

My body shook involuntarily. "I must be the most open book ever. How is it that you know what I was thinking?"

The grin. Then the smile. "Because I know myself. I also know that you are a good man. It is what any good man would think. No magic powers."

He pulled out two cigars. He cut a hole in each, then handed me one. We lit, and puffed in silence for a couple of minutes.

"I wanted to have a word with you alone," Max started. His cigar had a quarter inch of white-grey ash at the end. He held his cigar absent-mindedly.

I raised my eyebrows in reply.

"I've been watching you and your family. If you don't mind me saying, I am proud of you. And, you are a lucky man to have such a wonderful girl and wife."

"They are magnificent. I don't deserve them."

Max blinked and looked at me. "You didn't. But now you do. Just remember not to take them for granted."

"What am I supposed to say after that? I agree? Of course, I will not take them for granted."

"What you should take from it is that you didn't deserve them when they had one foot out the door. You lost what it was inside of you that made you who you are. When you rediscovered it, they saw it and returned. I don't know what you did or how you did it, but you are a very different man than the one I met in the cabin."

My mouth twitched. I didn't take compliments well. I think it was a compliment. I knew that he meant how I sorted out my non-financial mess.

"In my language," Max continued, "you have made yourself credit-worthy. You have taken my lessons to heart and have applied them. You are living on less than you earn. You are able to treat yourself from monies that you can afford. You have built a viable business with real prospects. Oh, yes, I have been keeping tabs on you. The burger vans were humble but they provided you with income, savings, and a launch pad to do what you are now doing. You understand how important the rules are—and how opportunity finds those who are ready. From what I can tell, you are earning a solid six figure income after tax and this is just the beginning."

I felt pulses of warmth through my chest. The pulses pushed themselves to my fingers and my toes. My cigar was clamped between my teeth and I said nothing.

"I met you today because I knew that you were ready. That you had evolved from the diffident man I met to a confident man with enough self-awareness to know what needs to be done."

"I am hardly infallible, Max," I said.

"I agree. None of us are. But you need to know what you don't know. And you do."

We both puffed our cigars. The ash had fallen from mine onto my jacket. I brushed it off. Luckily there was no breeze and even less traffic. The Thames drifted along indifferently as it had been doing so for tens of thousands of years before and would continue to do for tens of thousands of years after Max and I have been long forgotten.

"Let me cut to the chase. I want to invest in you. It will be sizeable. It is not a gift. You will need to pay me market interest rates plus a 25% stake in the venture."

My cigar almost fell out of my mouth. I expected a well-done speech. I expected the pat on the back. I knew that I had done well. I was in love with the most beautiful and wonderful woman in the world. And she, with me. We had a smart, feisty daughter with a real future ahead of her. The business was doing well. Finally. It was hard work. I had plans. I could expand. I would expand if I had enough capital.

"That's too kind, Max. I wasn't looking for this from you. We're friends. You always said that friendship and money don't mix."

"Yes. True. For most friends. But I am a business man. And you saved my grand-daughter. And I haven't really given you anything other than my advice. I was always going to give you something tangible. I was pleased that you never asked for it. And now that you are actually ready for it, I can kill two birds with one stone. I am always looking to employ my capital. You are in need of capital. And I am sorely in need of making some gesture to you that gives you a fraction of my appreciation for what you have done for me. You may need to accelerate your expansion plans, because I don't like to invest less than $50 million."

I found my voice. Everything was sharper. I could hear the sound of the tyres rolling on the tarmac next to us. The ripples on the water became suddenly apparent when, before, they had just merged into a drifting mass of grey. Birds appeared with their chirping. I didn't think that anything apart from pigeons and crows even lived in London. I looked at Max. I wanted to say something clever. Instead, all I could manage was, "Wow, thanks."

Max chuckled and put his massive hand on my shoulder and then patted it. "That's exactly what I said when it happened to me.

ABOUT THE AUTHOR

Baron made his first million by 30. Retired at 40. Began writing (notably, the <u>Man on The Run</u> series and <u>Migizi</u>) before returning to his business interests at 50. Wrote <u>Raindrops to Riches</u> when he realised what was really missing.

He is now semi-retired, writes, and is pursuing ventures that are wholly green, sustainable, and socially responsible. Baron aims to live life as set out in this book.

Baron was born in Canada. If not in the Surrey / Sussex Borders in the UK, he can be found in the South of France, near the Italian border. Alternatively, visit his site on <u>baronalexanderbooks.com</u>

www.ingramcontent.com/pod-product-compliance
Lightning Source LLC
Chambersburg PA
CBHW030529210326
41597CB00013B/1078